"From seeing the disappointment in your child's eyes when the other parent doesn't show up to dealing with your own disappointment when you can't fill all the empty spaces for your child, Lynda has been there. In *Single Moments,* she offers sensitive insights to single parents on how to handle the hurt and find healing. Her gentleness, honesty, and strength permeate these pages, offering single parents a three-fold cord of hope."

—Patsy Clairmont, speaker and author of *Sportin' A 'Tude*

"Blessed is the family that allows growing children to become who God wants them to be. Blessed are the parents who encourage that to happen as soon as possible and then get out of the way.

"*Single Moments* helps single parents do that. It is an outstanding tool for those pulling the load alone in a single harness."

—Barbara Johnson, author and speaker

"In the hurried and often weary world of single parenting, it helps when some-one who knows what you're going through can whisper words of hope and help in your ear. *Single Moments* offers sound bites of calm assurance from one of the nation's leading allies to single families."

—Dr. Tim Kimmel, author of *Raising Kids Who Turn Out Right*

"Lynda Hunter has emerged as the leading voice in the single-parent movement. She cares about the vast array of needs faced by single parents. What she has to say is built on personal, firsthand knowledge and wisdom—hers, and that collected from others. But most of all, her words come out of a godly character and a heart filled with love. There is no one more called or prepared to write to single parents than Lynda Hunter. I will be first in line to buy this book."

—Gary Richmond, pastor to single parents

"Discover hope and encouragement in Lynda Hunter's practical devotional for single parents. Sharing struggles, victories, joys, and sorrows, Lynda comes as a friend, offering both spiritual inspiration and practical how-tos for this challenging task of parenting. Honest, refreshing, inspiring, and equipping, Lynda Hunter's book is a *must* for every single parent."

—Linda McGinn, author, speaker, and "Keypoints" broadcaster

"Honest. Heart-touching. Encouraging. Personal. Lynda Hunter writes with profound vulnerability while providing practical, biblical alternatives to single parents faced with relational, financial, and spiritual challenges. With poignant illustrations based on her own experience as a single parent, Lynda reminds each of us that we are not alone. An extraordinary resource for men and women, *Single Moments* will help you maintain balance and stability as you face each day."

—Carol Kent, speaker and author of *Tame Your Fears* and *Detours, Tow Trucks, and Angels in Disguise*

Single Moments

Single Moments

Lynda Hunter, Ed.D.

TYNDALE

Tyndale House Publishers, Wheaton, Illinois

SINGLE MOMENTS
Copyright © 1997 by Lynda Hunter. All rights reserved.
International copyright secured.

Library of Congress Cataloging-in-Publication Data
Hunter, Lynda.
    Single Moments: a weekly devotional for single parents/Lynda Hunter.
      p. cm.
    ISBN 1-56179-532-1
    1. Single mothers—Prayer-books and devotions—English. 2. Single
parents—Prayer-books and devotions—English. 3. Devotional calendars.
I. Title.
BV4596.S48H86 1997
242'.6431—dc21   96-47495
                                                      CIP

A Focus on the Family Book Published by
Tyndale House Publishers, Wheaton, Illinois 60189

Unless otherwise noted, Scripture quotations are from the HOLY BIBLE, NEW
INTERNATIONAL VERSION ®. Copyright © 1973, 1978, 1984 by the International Bible Society. Used by permission of Zondervan Publishing House. All
rights reserved. Quotations labeled KJV are from the King James Version.

People's names and certain details of the case studies in this book have been
changed to protect the privacy of the individuals involved. However, the facts of
what happened and the underlying principles have been conveyed as accurately
as possible.

No part of this publication may be reproduced, stored in a retrieval system, or
transmitted in any form or by any means—electronic, mechanical, photocopy,
recording, or otherwise—without prior permission of the publisher.

Editors: Larry K. Weeden
Front cover design: Candi Park D'Agnese
Front cover photo: Richard Gaul/FPG International

Printed in the United States of America

00 01/10 9 8 7 6 5 4

Foreword

Admittedly, I'm not a single parent. But as I write this foreword to a wonderful book of weekly devotionals for single parents, I'm reminded of the single mom I loved most.

I was just two months old when my father left—too young to understand the gasp from my mother as she heard over the phone that Dad had "found somebody else" and wouldn't be coming back. For years, I would be too full of my own needs to realize Mom had heartaches and deep needs herself. And I would be too small to offer any help as she juggled school and work on top of loving and caring for *three* boys under the age of three (an older boy plus twins).

I have nothing but respect for the incredible job done by single parents. Growing up, I watched my mother struggle with the daily balance of working full-time while raising us boys. I saw her try to pay bills without ever receiving a child-support check. I marveled at how she so readily listened to our needs and hurts when she faced so many pressures herself. I wondered how she felt so at ease sleeping alone when the three of us boys always shared a room.

Don't get me wrong. My mom wasn't perfect. She lost it sometimes. She occasionally got angry. But through every up and down, *she had a secret source of strength.*

You'll read about that Source in this book. It's a Person who never failed her, always brought her comfort, walked with her down every trail, and dabbed every tear.

Mom discovered early in her single-parent journey what Lynda Hunter captures so well in this book. *Namely, you may be single, but you don't have to face a single day alone.* There's Someone who'll go with you each step of the way, who knows your hurts and needs even before you state them. That Someone can change you from the inside out and make life not just bearable, but streaked with joy and a purposeful future.

I can't urge you enough to soak in the wise, biblical counsel of this book. It's written by a woman I deeply respect who is herself a single parent—and has helped thousands of single parents through her work at Focus on the Family's *Single-Parent Family* magazine.

In closing, I don't think it was a coincidence that there was a message on the answering machine when we got home from dinner tonight. It was only a handful of words, spoken without emotion, but it caused an explosion of thoughts, feelings, and memories. "Dr. Trent," the voice said, "this is Paradise Memorial Gardens. We're just calling to let you know we set your mother's marker today."

I've stopped crying every day since my mom's recent death at the mention of her name. But I'll always remember her deep faith in the Lord Jesus. That "secret strength" stood in the gap in our home. He's the One who kept her strong and changed all our lives. Listen to a few words my brothers and I found tucked away in an old journal entry as we boxed up our mother's apartment:

"God has poured out blessings on me from the day of my birth. He has brought me to a wonderful church, and provided me an annotated Bible. All this plus the three miracles of creation who are my sons. How blessed could one woman be!"

How blessed you'll be as you spend time in these devotionals based on God's Word, discovering the hopeful future He has for you.

John Trent, Ph.D.
President, Encouraging Words

Introduction

As a young adult, I attended college in my hometown while living at home with six other siblings. Life was hectic, with all of us going in so many different directions. We shared clothes, food, and time with Mom and Dad. I was just one of the Hunter kids—nothing special most of the time.

My dad drove one of our two cars to work, while the second was divided among four other drivers. On alternating Fridays, Mom would deposit Dad's paycheck and head for the grocery store with clipped coupons in hand. At noon, she would pick me up from my classes at the university. We would grab a couple of double-decker hamburgers and drive home to eat lunch. My classes began again in the early afternoon, so our time together was brief.

Though I recall what we ate, it wasn't the burgers that were so memorable about those lunches. It wasn't our favorite box of chocolate cookies. It was those few minutes I got to spend alone with my mom. We talked and laughed and sometimes cried together. Mom heard about my classes, about boys I liked, and about my dreams. For those few minutes, time was frozen. No matter how many other kids Mom had, she was all mine, and I was all hers. Those were my single moments with my mother.

Others Had Them, Too

Throughout Jesus' life on earth, certain people sought single moments with Him as well amid His busy schedule. Matthew 8 begins with these words: "When he came down from the mountainside, large crowds followed him."

But Jesus had time for the individual. "A man with leprosy came and knelt before him and said, 'Lord, if you are willing, you can make me clean'" (verse 2).

What did Jesus do? He said, "I am willing. . . . Be clean!" (verse 3). That single moment with the busy Jesus brought life back to the man's dying body.

Jesus went on to Capernaum, about two miles away. He had many people to attend to, but a Roman soldier approached Him and asked Him to heal his paralyzed servant. Jesus did so from where He stood by speaking a single word.

Jesus' journey continued as He touched Peter's mother-in-law (see verse 14), two demon-possessed men (see verse 32), and a paralytic (see Matthew 9:2). Jesus also healed a woman who had been bleeding for 12 years (see Matthew 9:22) while on His way to raise the dead daughter of a young ruler (see Matthew 9:25).

Jesus walked with the masses. But to those He healed—those with leprosy, the servant, the mother-in-law, the woman, and the young girl—Jesus' ministry was an individual thing. Those whose lives were changed forever by His touch felt they were all that mattered during those single moments with Him.

Memories Still in the Making

It was late October, and darkness fell early. With dinner in the oven, my 10-year-old son and I drove to a favorite park nearby. He usually caught crayfish while I jogged and prayed in the woods. But the night was too cold for water creatures that evening, and the little light that was left didn't permit running.

I asked Clint if he wanted to go with me and see one of the places where I prayed. He nodded, so I challenged him to a race. A few minutes of laughter took us around the lake and up the path into the pines. Breathing hard, I led the way to a stump and sat down against the trunk of another tree. Clint plopped beside me as my left arm held him close for warmth.

"Let's give thanks to God for some things," I said. "I'll begin. Thank You, God, for letting us live in this beautiful country."

"Thank You for my tennis shoes," Clint said with a giggle.

"Thank You for keeping us well," I responded.

"Thank You for letting me play basketball and for all the things You do for us that we don't even know about," Clint said, his tone more serious.

Our dialogue became an emotional time of naming many things we knew God had done for us.

Soon the mountains in the distance were hard to discern in the darkness. Clint and I raced for the car. We returned to homework and phone calls and planning for the next day. But for that single moment, Clint had been mine and I had been all his no matter how many other children or responsibilities I had. We talked and laughed and wiped a tear or two.

I knew how Clint felt, because I had spent similar time just that morning with God. I talked to Him about the hardships I faced and people in my life. I smiled as I checked off the old list of prayers He had already answered, and I cried as I made a new list of problems I now faced.

When I spend those times alone with God, I know I'm more than just one of the Hunter kids. I know He understands. I know I can talk to Him about everything, and He cares about the matters that concern me. I know He won't condemn me for my failures. I know He'll always be there to meet my needs and to teach me what I should be learning.

The strength we all find to run life's race and to face new challenges depends on the regular single moments we spend with God. This book is designed to help you enjoy such moments. Read about the things that matter most, and memorize the ending Scripture verses, which will help you remember you are not alone. You are His, and He is yours—all yours! May God be with you as you find your single moments with Him.

1

An Ever-Faithful Partner

The child...
clutched her father's hand as they made their way across the street. The loud noise and fast movement did not matter as long as she stayed close to her father. She was small, and she skipped and giggled and sang. He was tall, and he took care of the rest.

The girl...
kissed her father good-bye as she left for a movie with a friend. When she returned, her father was waiting. They sat and talked and laughed.

The woman...
held her father's arm as they walked down an aisle toward the man she had chosen. Tears blinded her eyes as she turned from her father to her soon-to-be husband. She would look to him now to care for her and show her the love she needed.

The woman...
held the new baby daughter in her arms. She wondered at the miracle of birth and at the mystery of life. She and her husband loved, fed, cared for, and taught the little girl as she grew.

The woman...
held another daughter. She brought her close and felt immediate love for this second child, who was so different from the first. And then the woman learned that her father was very ill.

The woman . . .

held another child within her, a son. She looked forward to a family of five. But the husband said, "I have found someone else. I'll be leaving."

The woman . . .

sat on the floor. She watched the two little girls who slept peacefully in their beds, unsure of what was to follow. She felt the son growing inside her. Then she cried.

The woman . . .

did not know what to do. She looked around, and there was no one. Her husband was gone; her father was dying. She looked behind her and wondered where she had gone wrong. She looked in front of her and shook with fear at what lay ahead. And then she looked up to the God who had been there all along. "I need help," she told Him. "I give You my life and all I am. Take us and keep us a family."

The woman . . .

became a new bride that day. God took her and her little ones in His arms and held them there. He fed them. He clothed them. He loved them. And they were a family. "A father to the fatherless, a defender of widows, is God in his holy dwelling" (Psalm 68:5).

The woman . . .

found that her new Husband did not wander away. All that He told her in His Word was true. He provided for all her family's needs.

The children . . .

also got to know God. He became a father to them. He was always with them. They learned to depend on Him and to love Him as well. And they knew He would always be their Father.

The woman . . .

now looks around her and sees her Husband in all she does. She looks behind her, and what is there no longer matters. She looks in front of her and smiles at the future, though she still does not know what lies ahead. And then she looks up and says, "Thank You."

The events described here occurred several years ago, but, like ripples spreading out from a tiny rock thrown into a pond, I discover more of their results every day that I walk with Him.

I was raised in a Christian home, yet I never embraced a personal commitment to Christ. From those years, however, I remembered a Jamaican missionary who would come to my dad's church and sing a chorus from his native land. The song had a strange word in it, *Ishi* (pronounced "ee-shy"), and it went like this:

> *Ishi, Ishi, He's my jewel.*
> *Mine while endless ages roll.*
> *He's my altogether lovely.*
> *He's the Ishi of my soul.*

I would listen to the song, but I didn't know who Ishi was, and I didn't know about the relationship the words described. I watched how God answered prayer and solved problems in our family. But who He was and how He accomplished all that remained a mystery to me. He continued to be a distant image who loved the righteous and the good but hated sin and evil. I, therefore, pictured Him as a giant master over His slaves, leaving no room for explanations.

Then in the crisis of divorce, I became acquainted with Him for the first time. Getting to know Him in the years since has been a delight— and a relief. He moved into my life and took charge of all that concerned my family and me. As He accomplished this, I began to no longer see Him as the *master* of my life. Instead, I saw Him as the good *Husband* who had heretofore remained a myth to me.

Sometime later, I discovered a Scripture: "'In that day,' declares the Lord, 'You will call me "my husband"; you will no longer call me "my master"'" (Hosea 2:16).

With new enthusiasm, I began to study who "my husband" was. And then I found that the original Hebrew word for *husband* was one I had learned long before. It was *Ishi*.

Today, as I go about my day, I find myself singing the song I used to hear. Only now, I know both who Ishi is and how lovely a relationship with Him can be. He's the Ishi of my soul.

During your devotions, ask yourself, *Have I allowed God to become my Husband?* (Single fathers, this applies to you, too. Remember it was a man, Hosea, who wrote this passage after his wife, Gomer, left him.) God can become the Ishi to all of us.

❧ ❧ ❧ ❧ ❧ ❧ ❧ ❧

1. Name the qualities that characterize a good husband.

2. Describe ways in which one who has a good husband shows appreciation.

3. Any mate needs to spend time talking with his or her spouse and doing things together. That's when he or she gets to know the spouse best. List some ways you can become intimately acquainted with your heavenly Husband.

4. Finally, always remember that what's behind you no longer matters, and whatever lies ahead will be provided for by your Husband. That's worth a special "thank you." Take some time to lavish your love and gratitude upon Him in prayer.

"For your Maker is your husband—the Lord Almighty is his name" *(Isaiah 54:5).*

2

The Hidden Spot

The rays of the early morning sun were breaking through the clouds. I rose as the rest of the house remained captive to the silence. My steps were slow and my eyes were barely open because of the wakefulness of my small daughter through the night. But I had to spend some time with the Lord.

I walked into the room with the overstuffed chair. Tiny specks of lint danced in the rays of sunshine that streaked around the sides of the curtains. I picked up my Bible from the shelf, settled into the chair, and pulled the small cover around my bare legs.

"Good morning, Lord," I greeted. "Thank You for Your faithfulness. Thank You for my family's health and happiness, and for the provisions You send each day. Thank You for the things I don't see that You're also doing."

I rubbed more sleep from my eyes and continued with what I knew I should do. "God, there are so many I need to pray for—the Joneses and the problems in their marriage; the little boy down the street who is in the hospital; and my church, which struggles with new decisions and deeper reliance on You." I paused to think, stifling a yawn, and then went on.

"God, I just wanted to remind You of the dire needs in our home for which I keep praying. You know I have not received an answer yet, and Your Word promises me You will answer. I've prayed long and hard. I don't know what else to say. Do You really hear me? Do You care what's happening to me? Aren't You going to do anything to help me?"

I finished my prayer. With Bible replaced and cover folded, I went upstairs to awaken everyone for the new day. A busy morning followed of bathing, ironing, feeding, hugging, and sending out the door.

I spent the day with all those chores mothers do—the ones that soon have to be done all over again. As I worked, I thought about my small daughter. I wondered why she had started waking up in the night. There were no physical reasons, and I knew she felt secure. But her interruptions were beginning to take their toll on all of us. What was I going to do?

Soon I knew. I would just let her cry through the night and allow her to learn that Mom would not come in every time she called out. I hoped that would teach her to sleep soundly till morning.

The day went by swiftly. Dinner was finished, and story time was taking place. I snuggled with the children and read to them from *The Velveteen Rabbit*. I put them into their beds and kissed them good night.

Soon my opportunity came to follow my new plan. My sleep was disturbed by Courtney's whimpers. I heard her stand in the bed and shake the sides for a response. I slid from beneath the sheets and walked quietly to a hidden spot beside her door. I listened to her cry for much too long, until she finally lay back down and gave in to exhausted slumber. I gratefully climbed back into my own bed, feeling satisfied with my new late-night tactic.

I was sleeping soundly when Courtney awoke with another wail. I listened for signs of danger in her voice and again took my place beside her door, where she couldn't see. I remained there until she was sound asleep. Then I slipped to her side and pulled the covers up around her chin before returning to my room.

The third time Courtney awoke, I felt some anger as I lay still, hoping this crying spell would pass and she would go back to sleep without additional struggle. But once again, I moved toward her room, to the hidden spot beside her door. After peeking to be sure she was safe, I slid to the floor and rested my head against the wall. Her cries continued as she seemed to be saying, "Do you really hear me? Do you care what happens to me? Are you going to do anything to help me?"

Where have I heard these questions before? I wondered. And then I knew. I had sat inside my own groaning just that morning, crying out to my heavenly Father. In my despair, I had asked the same questions: "Do You really hear me? Do You care what happens to me? Are You going to do anything to help me?"

Courtney's cries muted to a whimper.

Could it be? I wondered. *Did God have His own hidden place just outside my room, where He stood watching over me while I prayed and cried to Him? Could it be He really did hear me cry, but He stood silent because I needed to learn something—something that would make me grow stronger? Could it be—of course it could—that God did not bat an eye or move from that hidden place till I was once again safe in the slumber of rest and release?*

I listened to the quiet of the sleeping child in the bed not far away. I also listened to the silent explanations from God. Then I returned to my own bed and pulled the covers up around me. A reassuring glance at the hidden place just outside my door made me smile.

My own whimpering subsided, and I closed my eyes to sleep.

All of us go through times when we pray and it seems as though God doesn't hear. Various people in the Bible also experienced such spiritually dry seasons. One such person was Joseph. Beginning in Genesis 37, we read his story.

Joseph was Jacob's favorite son. His brothers knew it, and it made them jealous. When Joseph was 17, they grabbed him and sold him to a group of Ishmaelites as a slave. The Ishmaelites took him to Egypt and sold him to Potiphar, an officer of Pharaoh, the king. Joseph worked there until Potiphar's wife tried to seduce him. When Joseph declined and fled, she told Potiphar he had attacked her.

Joseph, though once again innocent, was thrown into prison. He remained there until he was 30 years old—a total of 13 years in bondage. As we read the account, however, we don't find one place where he denied God—even to the end of the long years of seeming silence from the Lord. Then Pharaoh sent for Joseph to interpret a dream for him. "I cannot do it," Joseph replied to Pharaoh, "but God will give Pharaoh the answer he desires" (Genesis 41:16).

God stepped out of His hidden spot and brought deliverance to Joseph. He became Pharaoh's second-in-command, and as we read in the rest of Genesis, he saved Egypt and his family from famine and was eventually reunited with them.

You can be as certain as Joseph that deliverance will come. But you must be faithful to God and His Word even in difficult times when He seems not to be paying attention to you.

❧ ❧ ❧ ❧ ❧ ❧ ❧ ❧

1. Where was God through all of Joseph's trials? (Read Genesis 39:2 to find where God was while Joseph was in Potiphar's house. Read 39:21 to find where God was while Joseph was in prison for so many years.)

2. Though God was *with* Joseph, what was He doing *for* him during those trying times? (Read Genesis 39:3-6 and 22-23.)

3. In your own experience, what kinds of things have happened to you that you didn't deserve?

4. In what ways did the Lord seem silent when you went to Him with your needs?

5. Think hard and recount the ways you now realize God worked in your behalf from His hidden spot in your life.

6. God sometimes chooses to remain silent in order to build our faith. List as many ways as you can that your faith has grown through difficult times.

"What is seen is not made out of what was visible" (Hebrews 11:3).

3

No Fear

The single mother walked into the bedroom of the teenager who had left home—confused, rebellious, determined to find her own way. On her wall she had mounted various statements cut out of magazines:

"Live life as you see it."

"Play with fire. Skate on thin ice."

"Be good, be bad, just be."

Draped across the foot of her bed was a T-shirt the girl had hurriedly discarded. Her mom picked it up, and her fingers traced the letters branded across the chest: "No Fear."

She remembered the words the teenager had screamed at her. She recalled the heartbreak the girl had caused her dad. Respect for her parents, teachers, coaches, and adult relatives and friends had been replaced by a determination to make her own statements, set her own rules, and stretch her own boundaries.

No fear. It seems to be a popular theme in this generation.

Fear: The Kind God Doesn't Give Us

My seven-year-old daughter, Ashley, cried. She hadn't been able to sleep in her own bed for many nights. Every morning, I would find her snuggling close to me. "I'm afraid" is all she would tell me.

Ashley walked into her room one evening just as the breeze lifted her curtain. She screamed, and I came running. "Someone's in my room!" she claimed.

Weeks of working and praying closely with Ashley followed. We talked about the assurance of her physical safety. We talked about the assurance of being in God's care.

In the Bible, one Greek word for fear is *deilia*. It denotes cowardice and timidity—a kind of fear not given to us by God. In contrast, Jesus said, "Peace I leave with you; my peace I give you. I do not give to you as the world gives. Do not let your hearts be troubled and do not be afraid" (John 14:27).

Ashley eventually overcame her fearfulness at night. But when I would strip her bed sheets, I would find the little piece of paper hidden under her pillow, with the verse she had discovered about this *deilia* fear, written with a seven-year-old hand: "For God hath not given us the spirit of fear; but of power, and of love, and of a sound mind" (2 Timothy 1:7, KJV). She had exchanged the kind of fear God doesn't give for the sound mind and good sleep He does.

Fear: The Kind He Gives Us

When I was a teenager, I baby-sat for a family in our hometown. Their youngest son, Randy, was barely walking one afternoon when I joined him and his family around their grandparents' pool. My job was to watch Randy while I enjoyed the day. He toddled near the water, and the adults ruffled his blond, curly hair. Bravery and boldness marked his immature steps.

Suddenly the mood changed. The others walked away, and Randy plunged into the deep end of the pool. I called out, but no one heard.

There was no time to waste. Fully clothed, I jumped in. Though I wasn't a strong swimmer, I moved through the water with determination. Randy was floating upside down beneath the surface. I struggled and stretched until I pulled a gasping, sputtering one-year-old back to safety.

Randy cried and ran to his mother's arms for solace. Then he went about his play again—far from the edge of the pool. Randy took his bucket, truck, and newfound respect for the water to the safety of the chain link fence and stayed there the rest of the afternoon.

Similar to Randy's respect for the power of water, *eulabeia* means "reverence, or fear, of God." It mingles fear and love and results in the piety of a person toward God. It affects how we feel and the choices we make. In the Old Testament, this fear takes the form of dread, or terror. The New Testament speaks of a wholesome fear of displeasing God.

Today's generation is not the first to think fear is an emotion of the past. The Egyptians, who held God's people in bondage, taunted Moses and the Israelites by pitting their gods against the one true God of Israel. Then God sent plagues—each one for a different god in Egypt to prove to the Egyptians that He was greater. It finally put fear into the Pharaoh, and he let the people go.

But this Exodus lesson in fear didn't stop there. Subsequent generations of Israelites passed on that reverential fear to their children: "But the Lord, who brought you up out of the land of Egypt with great power and a stretched out arm, him shall ye fear, and him shall ye worship, and to him shall ye do sacrifice. . . . But the Lord your God ye shall fear; and he shall deliver you out of the hand of all your enemies" (2 Kings 17:36, 39, KJV).

Passing It On

Like the early Israelites, we need to show our kids an intense love for God, along with a deep, abiding, reverential respect for Him. How do we do that?

We begin when our children are small by teaching them to respect their parents and other significant adults. If they don't learn that, they'll have trouble respecting God when they're older. The teen I described earlier who left home confirmed that fact. Her mother told her once that she should respect her dad. The teen responded, "I can *show* respect, but I cannot *respect* him." That disrespect turned shortly on the mother and eventually manifested itself against God, too.

The hearts of our children can be taught respect and a healthy fear if we start early. We should earn and then require respect for adults while we're teaching them to fear God through Bible verses and the principles they involve. We also need to enforce appropriate consequences when they do not. "Show proper respect to everyone: Love the brotherhood of believers, fear God, honor the king" (1 Peter 2:17).

Recently my children and I stood around the kitchen counter eating breakfast. As we ate, we did a simple Bible study dealing with compromise. And as part of the discussion, one of my children challenged a family rule that prohibited her from going to a movie she wanted to see. She thought the rule was unfair and needed to change. I responded with all the justification I knew based on what we stood for. Then I stopped and, remembering my instruction to "teach your children the fear of the Lord" (Proverbs 1:7), said, "But you make some good arguments. Let's ask your Father what He thinks."

At that point I prayed, asking God to direct us and show us the right choices to make. Then we discussed the matter further, and she ended up not going to the movie.

My children won't forget Who we went to for guidance that morning and many others. They won't forget that what God thinks matters, and we will always stand on the principles He teaches. They will remember that our home does not endorse the "no fear" philosophy; rather, the proper fear of God guides all we do. That's a standard that will never change.

❄ ❄ ❄ ❄ ❄ ❄ ❄ ❄

Find ways to teach your children godly fear. Don't concentrate so much on disrespectful behavior, but pursue the beliefs that guide them.

Try several things:

• Read stories of God's overcoming power in the Bible. You can find them everywhere.

• Contrast the people in the Bible who trusted God with those who did not. Clarify what happened to them.

• Walk through today's choices with your kids. What fears do they have? Which of the fears are from God? Which are not? How can you tell the difference?

"Fear the Lord your God, serve him only and take your oaths in his name" *(Deuteronomy 6:13).*

4

The Manual

My children had left the day before to spend two weeks with their dad. I had a long list of catching-up things to do. Around dinner time, I received a phone call. A young woman from our church had been rushed to the hospital, and they asked if I would come to pray.

I spent the night at the hospital with a few others. This unmarried woman, who had gotten pregnant, was having a diabetic reaction. I watched her thrash and talk incoherently while the doctors fought to pull her through.

Returning home at dawn, I prepared for a slower day. But the phone rang once again. Another young girl I knew had tried to commit suicide. I jumped into the car once more and drove to an adjoining state. There I spent several hours with this beautiful young person whose stomach had had to be pumped.

On my trip home, my emotions ran high. In fact, I hit the steering wheel with my hand in anger as I thought about what had gone wrong for both of those young women. Neither had grown up in a Christian home. Though both knew something about the Lord through attending church in their recent years, neither had those beginning foundations.

I found myself thinking, *Any appliance comes with a manual. It tells us how to assemble the appliance, how to maintain it, and how to fix it if something goes wrong. God has given us parents a manual—the Bible—for life, including how to raise our kids. So what are we missing?*

The Joshua Decision

My thinking led me in time to the biblical book of Joshua. This man had a vibrant relationship with God. He looked to Him for every decision he made and every direction he took. He found God faithful through good times and bad.

His faith did not remain his own, either. He shared it with the people of Israel he was called to lead. He reminded them of their heritage and identity. He set up standing stones after they crossed the Jordan River that God had rolled back so they could enter the Promised Land. He told the people, "In the future, when your children ask you, 'What do these stones mean?' tell them that the flow of the Jordan was cut off before the ark of the covenant of the Lord. . . . These stones are to be a memorial to the people of Israel forever" (Joshua 4:6-7).

Joshua encouraged those under him much as we do with our own children. I tell my kids how God miraculously provided the money to pay a bill or gave me the job I needed. These "standing stones" remain as memorials to our children about how we looked to God and He came through.

Another thing Joshua did was to teach his people God's statutes. "There was not a word of all that Moses had commanded that Joshua did not read to the whole assembly of Israel, including the women and children, and the aliens who lived among them" (Joshua 8:35).

I started long ago teaching my kids why we conduct our lives as we do. One day my daughter was having trouble with one of her friendships at school. I didn't just give her an answer, but together with her brother and sister, we looked up all the scriptures about friends that we could find.

Then we listed the qualities of a friend on a chalkboard—"loveth at all times," "is friendly," "should be equally yoked."

Next, we named the person in question. Did she meet God's standards for a friend?

Finally, we examined *ourselves* to see how we stacked up.

This simple exercise answered a small question for a child on a particular day. But much more than that, she was encouraged to grow in a vibrant, consistent trust in God that will sustain her in the days and years to come.

Just before Joshua died, he delivered a farewell address. He told the people to remember the manual—God's Word—which had taught them everything they needed to know. Then he said it was time for them to choose whom they were going to serve. They had watched him serve the Lord, and many of them had done the same, but now the decision to go on would be theirs alone.

Those Who Followed

We read in Judges 2:7, "The people served the Lord throughout the lifetime of Joshua and of the elders who outlived him and who had seen all the great things the Lord had done for Israel."

Unfortunately, however, the people of that generation failed to pass on their faith to their sons and daughters, who had not witnessed firsthand many of God's great works on behalf of Israel. For that new generation, their relationship with God was not vibrant and personal. So guess what happened to them?

"After that whole generation had been gathered to their fathers, another generation grew up, who knew neither the Lord nor what he had done for Israel" (Judges 2:10).

This generation had not been raised according to God's manual. They had not been taught how to assemble their lives, how to maintain them, or how to fix them when something went wrong. Consequently, they conducted their lives independent of God's commands and directions.

The Choice

Our lives are full of choices. But the most important one we will ever make is to serve God and trust Him for more than just a Sunday morning trip to church. The decision to make Him the center of our daily existence shapes both our lives and those of our kids.

God gives us a manual in the Bible to show us how to live. If we don't read it or follow its principles (like me with my appliance manuals), things get fouled up and we don't know what to do. But when we understand God's precepts and pass them on to our children, we get what Jesus called an abundant life.

My kids and I were leaving church one Sunday night when an older couple stopped to talk to us. I told them I was without a job and didn't know how we were going to pay our bills.

We drove on home and prepared for bed. I was sitting on the edge of my bed when I heard the door creak open. In walked my older daughter, who hugged me and placed something in my hand.

I opened the folded piece of paper and read, "Trust for Mom's job." Written below were three Bible verses my daughter had looked up to remind me to trust in God's complete sufficiency.

I wish I had learned the lesson about trusting Him as well as she had. That night, I needed to go back to the manual and fix the things that had gone wrong. What a wonderful reminder from a daughter who is choosing this day to serve the Lord!

✄ ✄ ✄ ✄ ✄ ✄ ✄ ✄

1. What natural environment do you use to teach your children the Bible?

2. To what extent do you model what it means to build your life according to the principles of God? How do you do that?

3. Schedule workable times in your home for maintaining individual walks with God through regular prayer and Bible study.

4. List ways you can show your children how to fix things according to His teachings when they go wrong.

"Only be careful, and watch yourselves closely so that you do not forget the things your eyes have seen or let them slip from your heart as long as you live. Teach them to your children and to their children after them" (Deuteronomy 4:9).

5

In God We Trust?

We were driving down the highway when my daughter asked about the simple words printed on a coin in her hand. "What does it mean, Mom, 'In God We Trust'?"

I said the words were chosen years ago to represent our country's belief system. I explained how our nation was founded on biblical principles, but that as the years passed we turned our backs on the simple beliefs that had formed our foundation. And each generation knew a little less and questioned a little more the meaning of "In God We Trust."

Sounds Familiar

As I talked to my daughter, I couldn't help but think about my own history of trust in God. I was raised in a Christian home, but as a child I never became personally acquainted with the Lord. Instead, I enjoyed the blessings of God indirectly through my parents' reliance on Him.

My lack of commitment worked as long as I was under my parents' roof. But as I grew up and struck out on my own, I found myself standing in a puddle of compromise. My identity appeared no different from that of others around me who made no claim to be Christians.

Compromise became my way of life. It didn't happen all in one day. Rather, it occurred little by little, one decision at a time. Then I met my husband-to-be, who knew nothing of the things of the Lord. Life seemed to be going okay, and I never thought I would need God more in the days to come than I felt I did on the blissful day I said "I do." Though the absence of spiritual matters in my marriage was difficult to adapt to at first, I did just that—I adapted.

We moved into a small house on his family's horse farm. When my husband would enter the house from the barn, I found the animal stench on his clothes repulsive. But over time, I became immune to the smell. Then one day my sister came to visit, and she put on *my* barn jacket to step outside. Unable to bear the offensive odor, she quickly pulled the jacket back off. It dawned on me then that my husband didn't stink to me anymore because I smelled just like him, both physically and spiritually.

The Need for Something More

I filled the void inside me with busyness and devotion to the man I had married. I looked to him to be all things. Our church attendance was sporadic, and none of our decisions were made with God in mind.

Then I became pregnant, and I started asking myself, *What spiritual things should I impart to my child?* Something began to gnaw at my insides, and I grew hungry to know the God of my parents.

One Sunday afternoon in June, soon after we learned I was pregnant, my husband and I set out to mow some horse trails along the river for a group trail ride the following weekend.

I climbed onto the fender above the left wheel of the tractor as my husband drove across the ragged juts in the field next to our home. I was holding firmly to the seat, enjoying the early summer air, when I seemed to hear from nowhere a Bible verse I had learned long ago: "God is our refuge and strength, an ever-present help in trouble" (Psalm 46:1).

The words rang in my ears, but my attention was drawn back to the task at hand. We headed down a gravel road toward the river. Once we entered the wooded area, my husband turned on the bushhog and began mowing the weeds. Soon we pulled into some ragweed that reached around the sides of the tractor and cut our legs. My husband asked me to run back to the house and get our jeans to protect us from further discomfort.

I jogged to the house, pulled on some jeans, and tied a pair for my husband around my waist. I soon arrived back at the river bottom and followed the sound of the tractor engine and busy bushhog. I found my husband out of the ragweeds, making a clear path down the trail. He helped me back above the left tire.

We entered a dense part of the woods where the trees blocked the sunlight. Just as we rounded a curve in the path, a back tire of the tractor rolled onto a large mound of dirt hidden by wooden debris. The tractor tipped. I grabbed for a handhold, but I lost my balance and was flung toward the ground. *Move away from the tractor,* I thought. But as I dropped through the air, the rotating tire I had been seated above grabbed the jeans tied around my waist. I was pulled underneath as the tractor came down on all four wheels.

I peered around frantically. Gripped with fear, I focused through tears on the bushhog going behind and gasoline dripping in front. Under the weight of the tractor, I couldn't feel my right hip and ankle, and I could see only blood—my blood—soaking the ground around me. *My baby!* I thought. *What's going to happen?*

I looked up at my husband. "Pleeeease help," I pleaded. But the man who had replaced God in my life sat above in utter helplessness, moving the gears this way, then that. He finally rolled the tractor off of me, and I dragged myself to the other side of the path.

I lay on the damp ground, the smell of earth surrounding me. I felt intense pain as warm blood drenched my clothes. I feared for the damage that had been done both to me and my child.

From that spot on the ground, the only way to look was up. I lifted my gaze high above where the tree branches parted, revealing the bright blue sky. Then I heard as clearly as any words ever spoken to me, "God is our refuge and strength, an ever-present help in trouble."

I became aware of the presence of God, and I knew somehow everything was going to be all right. I blinked back the tears once again, but this time not in fear. "God, forgive the sins in my life," I prayed. "Will You come into my heart and become the One in whom I can place my trust from this day forward?"

And so it was: The Scripture was fulfilled that says, "Everyone who calls on the name of the Lord will be saved" (Acts 2:21).

The Days to Come

Eight months later, our healthy baby girl was born. My broken ankle had long since healed, and the wounds on my hip had disappeared. But nothing in my life was the same after that afternoon in the woods when I realized no thing or person would ever be able to fill the place in my life that belonged solely to God. I had not earned His favor, and I certainly didn't deserve it, but He knew right where to find me that summer afternoon.

The years that followed brought two more children and more times of trouble. Ultimately, my husband left us completely. New problems to solve and decisions to make brought me time and again to that spot beneath the wheels of the tractor where I realized I had no one to turn to but God.

I hear other individuals tell about the places and events that have put them "under the tractor wheel." They, like I, have realized how people and things count for nothing when God is forgotten. People will disappoint you, and your expectations will often be dashed. But God—and only God—promises, "Never will I leave you; never will I forsake you" (Hebrews 13:5). His continued faithfulness to that promise has taught my daughter and me the true meaning of "In God We Trust."

We sometimes make the most basic act of the Christian faith—asking Jesus Christ to save us—a much more difficult process than God ever intended it to be. Jesus illustrated the simplicity of it in a conversation with Nicodemus (John 3:1-21).

Nicodemus was a rabbi, a member of the Jewish ruling council and one of the richest men in Jerusalem. One night, he came to Jesus. Here's what they said.

Nicodemus: "Rabbi, we know you are a teacher who has come from God. For no one could perform the miraculous signs you are doing if God were not with him."

Jesus: "I tell you the truth, no one can see the kingdom of God unless he is born again."

Nicodemus: "How can a man be born when he is old? Surely he cannot enter a second time into his mother's womb to be born!"

Jesus: "No one can enter the kingdom of God unless he is born of water and the Spirit. Flesh gives birth to flesh, but the Spirit gives birth to spirit. . . . You must be born again. The wind blows wherever it pleases. You hear its sound, but you cannot tell where it comes from or where it is going. So it is with everyone born of the Spirit."

Nicodemus: "How can this be?"

Jesus: "Just as Moses lifted up the snake in the desert, so the Son of Man must be lifted up, that everyone who believes in him may have eternal life."

How do you become born again? "If you confess with your mouth, 'Jesus is Lord,' and believe in your heart that God raised him from the dead, you will be saved" (Romans 10:9).

Find a quiet place to talk to God. Tell Him you believe that Jesus died for your sins and then rose from the grave to be your Savior. Ask Him to forgive your sins and come into your heart—to take over your life! It's as simple as that.

He will wash away your sins and make you as clean and spotless as a newborn baby. Every sin you have ever committed will be removed "as far as the east is from the west" (Psalm 103:12).

Then, as a child grows through eating good foods and receiving nurturing care, you should grow in the Lord through reading the Bible, praying, getting close to other believers, and learning to place your trust in God.

❧ ❧ ❧ ❧ ❧ ❧ ❧ ❧

Use the following to help you remember to trust in God daily:

T—Talk with other believers.
List those you know who also trust in God and could build your faith.

R—Renew your vows to follow Him all your life.
Take this moment to tell God how much you love Him and how committed you are to Him always.

U—Uncover His promises by reading the Bible every day.
Go to the concordance of your Bible. Write down all the scriptures you can find about trust.

S—Stand firm on what these promises say by memorizing them. *Commit to memory all the verses you discovered. Do the same for any topic with which you're dealing. This is a sure-fire trust builder!*

T—Time with God is the best-spent time of your day! *From today on, set a time that suits you best, and make a daily appointment with God. Then don't let anything interrupt that commitment. You will be surprised at what you see take place.*

"Blessed is he whose help is the God of Jacob, whose hope is in the Lord his God" (Psalm 146:5).

6

Heart to Heart

Because I was born on Valentine's Day, I've had many memorable birthdays through the years. I vividly recall the heart-shaped cake pans my mom pulled from the cupboard as February approached and the ice cream treats we made for my classmates from heart-shaped cookie cutters and topped with red sprinkles. My white dress had red heart pockets of descending sizes on the skirt, and I got a sweet-16 silver heart charm for my bracelet.

I felt pretty special surrounded by all those hearts, secretly deciding that much of the hoopla on February 14 every year was held in my honor.

It's amazing how often the word *heart* figures in everyday life. In sixth grade, *I learned by heart* the Preamble to the Constitution, which I can still recite today. I recall a near burglary that left my *heart in my mouth*. When I was 17, *I found it in my heart* to give my last two dollars to a destitute man on the street. In college, I *took to heart* my education, putting myself through school and *having in my heart* the goal of earning a degree. I can still feel the *heartburn* of pregnancy, eating *heartily* during years of holidays, feeling *heartsick* when my dog was killed, watching *heartrending* movies, experiencing *heartaches* through many of life's disappointments, and finally *having my heart broken* on the path that brought me again to singleness.

"My Own Heart"

The *heart* means many things to many people. Webster tells us it is the seat of physical life and affections and the center of moral, intellectual, and spiritual life. Not until my husband left and my heart was truly broken did I *surrender my heart* and life to Jesus Christ. Only then and in the months following did I discover other meanings of *heart*.

Remember the story about God sending the prophet Samuel to Jesse's home to find the next king of Israel? Samuel looked at all the strong, handsome, obvious choices in the lineup of Jesse's sons. But God told Samuel in 1 Samuel 16:7 not to look at the externals because "the Lord looks at the heart." Then God chose David, someone He had already identified in 1 Samuel 13:14 as "a man after my own heart."

As children of God, our lifelong challenge is to become men and women after God's own heart. How do we ever reach such a goal?

Folded Together

As a child, I would cut out Valentine hearts to send to family and friends. But no matter how hard I tried, I couldn't find a way to cut a perfect heart. Then I discovered that I could take one side of a predrawn heart and fold it over onto a blank piece of paper, providing a pattern. Using that pattern, I could create a perfect heart.

As single parents, we live in a world that often equates singleness with being alone, broken, and rejected. But I'm encouraged by two Greek words the Bible uses to define the word *single:*

> *pleko*—"to twine, braid, or plait"
> *haplous*—"folded together"

Yes, loneliness, brokenness, and rejection are involved in being single. But we don't have to go it alone. In becoming single-hearted, we can be twined, braided, and folded over in Christ. *That* can show us the way to lasting love and joy.

Whether we're married or single is not the crucial issue. Rather, the key question is do we have singleness of heart with the Lord? When we do, we become men and women after His own heart, and our relationship can grow and mature.

For any relationship to develop, however, the two people must spend time together, engage in meaningful communication, and get to know everything they can about each other. Likewise, we must spend time with the Lord by being in church and finding Christian fellowship. We should engage in regular conversation with Him through prayer. And we need to learn all we can about Him through reading His Word. Then we will learn not only how to be single (folded and braided) in heart with the Father, but also how to remain there.

❖ ❖ ❖ ❖ ❖ ❖ ❖ ❖

1. Remember how you felt when you were in love and gave your heart to someone? What kind of change did that new love bring in your appearance? conduct? devotion? faithfulness? happiness? love? purity? sincerity? tenderness? trust?

2. As time went on and your new love became mature love, did those areas remain the same? What became different? Did those changes affect your overall relationship?

3. Unlike many natural relationships we develop, entering a supernatural relationship with God is forever. We'll make mistakes and falter. But God's Word is the pattern to "fold over" onto our lives. When we face mistakes, difficulties, or questions, we can go to the Bible and find clear direction.

Look up the following passages of Scripture. What instructions do they give you in the same areas of your life listed in question 1?

Appearance (1 Peter 3:3-4)

Conduct (1 Thessalonians 3:13; 1 Kings 8:61)

Devotion (Psalm 73:25; 77:6; 119:10)

Faithfulness (1 Kings 19:18; Revelation 17:14)

Happiness (Psalm 4:7; Jeremiah 15:16)

Love (Matthew 22:37; 1 John 4:16)

Purity (Matthew 5:8; 1 Timothy 1:5; 1 Peter 1:22)

Sincerity (Hebrews 10:22)

Tenderness (Ephesians 4:32)

Trust (Psalm 9:9, 40:4; 125:1; Proverbs 3:5; 14:26; 28:25; Isaiah 26:3)

4. I recently found a verse on an old Valentine's card that went something like this:

> *"Though my intentions are the best, so often all year through I know there are lots of things I fail to say or do. But you know you mean more to me than words can ever say. I want to say 'I love you' with all my heart today."*

Take some time today to send the Lord your valentine. Let Him know how much you want singleness of heart with Him. Tell Him all the special things you have intended to say all year through. Then listen, and let Him tell you just how much you are loved.

"Love the Lord your God with all your heart and with all your soul and with all your strength" (Deuteronomy 6:5).

7

Stop—and Keep Going

One Friday night last fall, the clock in my car said 9:17, and I was still going strong with my chores. Exiting the interstate, I turned right just in time to see a police officer, who also saw me. His light came on as he made a quick U-turn and hurried up behind me. I eased to the side of the road, and he parked behind me and then walked to my car.

"Ma'am," he said, "I pulled you over because you didn't come to a dead stop back at that stop sign. I'm going to give you a warning this time. But just remember, if you don't start making complete stops, you're going to have to pay a fine later on."

The following day, I was up by 4:00 to accomplish my household responsibilities—dinner in the crockpot, instructions to the children on schedules to follow—before heading to a seminar I would conduct. As I got in the car, I leaned my head against the headrest and sighed, already tired though the sun was barely up. Then I remembered the words of the officer from the night before: "If you don't start making complete stops, you're going to have to pay."

I needed to take time every day to stop, look around, establish my direction, and check for safety. But how does a single parent do this amid the stress of everyday life?

Stress comes in two varieties. Some, obviously, is bad—conflicts with former mates, money problems, unexpected repairs. Other sources of stress are actually positive—soccer games, birthday parties, holidays. But while the mind knows the difference, the wear and tear on the body is the same. Heart rate and blood pressure go up, brain activity is altered, and adrenaline appears in the bloodstream.

Taking Control of Stress

I realized some time ago that I don't often have control over the amount or kind of stress that enters my life, but I *do* have power over my reactions to it. So now when I'm up against it, I run through what I call my STRESS list to help me cope.

Sleep, rest, quiet time. "In vain you rise early and stay up late, toiling for food to eat—for he grants sleep to those he loves" (Psalm 127:2).

As the officer told me that night, we often need to come to complete stops. You and I require a solid night's sleep every night, in addition to rest breaks during the day.

Time management. "For there is a proper time and procedure for every matter" (Ecclesiastes 8:6).

I gain control in this area by first taking an inventory of my present use of time. Second, I concentrate on the task at hand by screening out distractions; I take the phone off the hook or get up early to accomplish a task. This also helps me to distinguish between the essentials and the nonessentials. Third, I grasp the big picture. I try to "major on the majors" and relate daily tasks to long-range goals. Fourth, I delegate those things that can be done by others, such as help with my housework. Finally, I prioritize. The main thing is to keep the main thing the main thing.

Routine exercise. "Don't you know that you yourselves are God's temple and that God's Spirit lives in you?" (1 Corinthians 3:16).

When I lived in Ohio, I loved to ride a 28-mile bike trail. But I went about it the wrong way, tackling the entire route only about every two months. That actually did more harm to my body than good.

Consistent, moderate exercise strengthens the heart, improves circulation, lowers cholesterol, helps to control weight, and reduces hypertension in addition to helping us cope with stress.

Eat healthy. "But Daniel resolved not to defile himself with the royal food and wine, and he asked the chief official for permission not to defile himself this way. . . . 'Give us nothing but vegetables to eat and water to drink.' . . . At the end of the ten days they looked healthier and better nourished than any of the young men who ate the royal food" (Daniel 1: 8, 12, 15).

Too often when we suffer the greatest stress and are the most hurried, we eat poorly and pass these habits on to our children. Good eating includes regular helpings of cereals, grains, fruits, vegetables, dairy products, and protein, along with a reduction in sugar and fat. To combat stress, eat plenty of foods containing vitamin B (whole grains, eggs, nuts, lean meats) and vitamin C (citrus fruits; green, leafy vegetables). On the other hand, caffeine increases susceptibility to stress, makes one irritable, disrupts sleep, and destroys vitamins B and C.

Socialize. "Let us not give up meeting together, as some are in the habit of doing, but let us encourage one another" (Hebrews 10:25).

As single parents, it is easy to neglect spending time with other adults. But we each need to find our relaxing spots—doing things and being with people we really enjoy. This time can be spent in worship, Christian fellowship, or just plain fun.

We also need to remember to have fun with our kids. When I was a new single parent, we moved to another state and settled into an apartment. I began my doctoral program while teaching, finishing the divorce, and leaving the children in a day-care center for the first time. In the midst of my busyness, I reserved one day to go to the zoo with my older daughter's kindergarten class. Three times that morning while we were getting dressed, Ashley said, "Mom, laugh and tell jokes today."

I finally heard what she was really saying: *Mom, you haven't been much fun lately. I need to see that side of you again.*

And I needed it, too.

Strengthen spiritual commitment. "Come near to God and he will come near to you" (James 4:8).

Not long ago, I realized it was as essential for me to go into my prayer closet in the morning and get equipped for the day as it was for me to get dressed from my clothes closet. Then at the end of the day, I find it refreshing to lie on my bed and talk to God. I ask Him what we should do about a bill I can't pay and to help me be more patient with the children. It's during the most difficult times of my life that I have drawn the closest to Him and Him to me.

God's Provision

I will always be amazed at the precision of God's plan. All living creatures experience stress, but He equips us to stand up under the challenges and even makes us better through them.

God created the oyster with a special product called *nacre* that goes to work when an invading substance, like a grain of sand, enters the shell. To protect the oyster's soft inner flesh, the foreign substance is coated with thin sheets of nacre in successive circular layers until it is completely enclosed, forming a pearl. The pearl takes on the same luster and color as the lining of the shell. If that lining is dull, the pearl will also be without luster and have no value.

Stress invades our lives like grains of sand. It pushes us out of our comfort zone and forces us to react. If we're wise, we let it push us right into the arms of God.

Stress is a necessary by-product of our everyday living. We don't want to eliminate it, because it causes us to develop maturity and character. But we *do* need to manage it better, to handle well the grains of sand that enter our shells. Who knows? We just may watch those invaders grow it into something of beauty and maturity in us—lustrous pearls that we might not otherwise have known.

A Biblical Model

Elijah was a man who knew stress. In 1 Kings 19, he was running from Queen Jezebel and King Ahab, who were trying to kill him. He ran into the wilderness and sat down under a broom tree, where he prayed. "I have had enough, Lord," he said. "Take my life" (verse 4). Then what happened?

He *slept.* "He lay down under the tree and fell asleep" (verse 5).

He spent the *time* for his good and developed a *routine.* "He ate and drank and then lay down again" (verse 6).

He obeyed the Lord's command to *eat* good foods. "All at once an angel touched him and said, 'Get up and eat . . . for the journey is too much for you'"(verses 5, 7).

He *socialized,* because he found a friend. "So Elijah went from there and found Elisha" (verse 19).

He grew *spiritually.* "The Lord said, 'Go out and stand on the mountain in the presence of the Lord, for the Lord is about to pass by'" (verse 11).

And the most beautiful part of it all? Elijah found what he needed from God in "a gentle whisper" (verse 12). God is not in the stresses of our lives. But He is ready to uphold us and guide us through them. And He resides in the quiet places where, like Elijah, when we finally come to a complete stop, we can hear what He has to say.

1. What can you do to develop better habits in each of the following areas?

sleep

time management

routine exercise

eating healthfully

socializing

spiritual growth

2. Make a list of quiet places you can add to your life. God is waiting to meet with you there.

"There remains, then, a Sabbath rest for the people of God; for anyone who enters God's rest also rests from his own work, just as God did from his. Let us, therefore, make every effort to enter that rest" (Hebrews 4:9-11).

8

The Empty Chair

A recent spring brought few signs of new life for me and many reminders of some severe trials my family had just gone through. I prayed, planned strategy, and agonized over how to respond to every detail of the challenge I faced, but it seemed I had failed. Not only were successes hard to find, but I had no strength left to try again.

In March, all my children went back to visit their dad for a week. Exhausted and depleted, I borrowed the empty apartment of a friend and made my way into the mountains. I stopped for an early lunch and a trip through an outdoor mall. I arrived at my destination in the early evening.

After unloading my luggage, my real time of unloading began. I sat on the living room couch, put a chair in front of me on the other side of the room, and imagined God sitting there. I needed for Him to feel tangible to me that night. Then I asked, "Why have You allowed all this to happen? Why don't You deliver us from these circumstances? Why?"

But I felt as if He didn't hear. My questions and explanations seemed to bounce off the wall much as they did for C. S. Lewis in his book *A Grief Observed:* "But go to Him when your need is desperate, when all other help is vain, and what do you find? A door slammed in your face, and a sound of bolting and double bolting on the inside. After that, silence. You may as well turn away. . . . What can this mean? Why is He so present a commander in our time of prosperity and so very absent help in time of trouble?"

Obviously, I wasn't the first who seemed to speak to an empty chair.

Job

Job asked similar questions in Job 23. He suffered with boils over his body and the loss of his home, cattle, land, seven sons, and three daughters. He cried out, "Even today my complaint is bitter; his [God's] hand is heavy in spite of my groaning" (verse 2).

This man knew what it was like to go through hard times. Like me, he had suffered pains that seemed unfair and unexplained.

"If only I knew where to find him [God]; if only I could go to his dwelling! I would state my case before him and fill my mouth with argument. I would find out what he would answer me, and consider what he would say" (verses 3-5).

Job must have stared at an empty chair as he said, "But if I go to the east, he is not there; if I go to the west, I do not find him. When he is at work in the north, I do not see him; when he turns to the south, I catch no glimpse of him" (verses 8-9).

Then something changed—no, not his circumstances. Something changed in Job. He remembered that the chair is never empty, and he spoke with fresh hope: "But he knows the way that I take; when he has tested me, I will come forth as gold" (verse 10).

We read further in this book of the Bible how God did, indeed, hear His servant's prayer and restore him. The new beginning didn't come that day, but the change in Job did, and that opened a pathway through which God could work.

David

The Bible speaks of David as a man after God's heart. Yet he was often in a pit of despair and looked for God from there:

"I cried out to God for help; I cried out to God to hear me. When I was in distress, I sought the Lord; at night I stretched out untiring hands and my soul refused to be comforted. I remembered you, O God, and I groaned; I mused, and my spirit grew faint" (Psalm 77:1-3).

David was lost in his misery. He searched everywhere for answers from God.

"You kept my eyes from closing; I was too troubled to speak. I thought about the former days, the years of long ago; I remembered my songs in the night. My heart mused and my spirit inquired: 'Will the Lord reject us forever? Will he never show his favor again? Has his unfailing love vanished forever? Has his promise failed for all time? Has God forgotten to be merciful? Has he in anger withheld his compassion?'" (Psalm 77:4-9).

Notice the personal pronouns David used. Twenty times in the first six verses, he loaded his prayer with words like *I, my, me,* and *mine.* He was consumed with his problems.

Boy, can I identify! The furthest thing from my mind that night in prayer was applauding God or interceding for someone else.

But then David remembered that the chair in his desperate room was filled with an awesome God, and his despair changed to praise. "Your ways, O God, are holy. What god is so great as our God? You are the God who performs miracles; you display your power among the peoples. With your mighty arm you redeemed your people, the descendants of Jacob and Joseph" (Psalm 77:13-15).

David had rediscovered the source of his strength and power.

Jeremiah

Another man cried so much that he earned a nickname, "the weeping prophet."

I am the man who has seen affliction by the rod of his wrath. He has driven me away and made me walk in darkness rather than light; indeed, he has turned his hand against me again and again, all day long. He has made my skin and my flesh grow old and has broken my bones. He has besieged me and surrounded me with bitterness and hardship. He has made me dwell in darkness like those long dead. (Lamentations 3:1-6)

Jeremiah went on to blame God for walling him in, weighing him down, keeping him in darkness, barring his way, making his paths crooked, and dragging, mangling, and leaving him without hope. "I remember my affliction and my wandering, the bitterness and the gall. I well remember them, and my soul is downcast within me" (Lamentations 3:19-20).

As long as Jeremiah dwelled on his troubles, everything seemed hopeless. But then, like Job and David, Jeremiah stopped pitying himself and remembered who he served.

Yet this I call to mind and therefore I have hope: Because of the Lord's great love we are not consumed, for his compassions never fail. They are new every morning; great is your faithfulness. I say to myself, "The Lord is my portion; therefore I will wait for him." The Lord is good to those whose hope is in him, to the one who seeks him; it is good to wait quietly for the salvation of the Lord. (Lamentations 3:21-26)

He Is There for Us

Job, David, and Jeremiah made conscious decisions to look to God. They declared their faith in Him. They recalled ways in which He had moved in the past. They praised Him for His strength and ability to restore. And when they did, things began to change.

In my crying-out place that March, I finished every desperate prayer

I could think of using every personal pronoun I knew. Then I began to thank Him. I lay on the couch and wrote out many of the things I had seen Him do. I listed the ways He had remained faithful to us through the years. The problems were not lessened, but I became convinced that they were in God's hands. This realization allowed me to go out the next morning onto a ski slope and spend the day enjoying something I love.

I was home by 6:30 that evening. Exhausted, I lay across my bed and remembered more of the words of C. S. Lewis: "Aren't all these notes the senseless writhings of a man who won't accept the fact that there is nothing we can do with suffering except to suffer it? Who still thinks there is some device (if only he could find it) which will make pain not be pain? It doesn't really matter whether you grip the arms of the dentist's chair or let your hands lie in your lap. The drill drills on."

I closed my eyes to sleep as the drill drilled on, but this time with my hands relaxed in my lap. I would always be okay, because that chair would never be empty. What a blessed assurance that is!

❧ ❧ ❧ ❧ ❧ ❧ ❧ ❧

1. Find a place where you can empty every burden in your heart before God. It may be in the car, on your bed, or in your church sanctuary. But tell Him all about it.

2. After you've finished, thank Him for everything you can remember that He has done for you.

3. Then go do something fun. The burden is the Lord's! There's no sense in two of you carrying it.

"Know that the Lord has set apart the godly for himself; the Lord will hear when I call to him" (Psalm 4:3).

9

The Emperor's New Clothes

Since childhood, I have enjoyed Hans Christian Andersen's story "The Emperor's New Clothes." It tells about an emperor whose only concern was for his attire. He could be found throughout the day, not in council chambers, but in his dressing room trying on clothes.

One day two tailors came to town who claimed they could make beautifully colored and patterned clothes visible to all—except those who were unfit for public service or who were very stupid.

The emperor ordered some new clothes from these tailors. After a time, he sent his prime minister to see how the clothes were coming along. When the prime minister arrived, he saw an empty loom and the tailors working with invisible needles. But he thought, *I certainly don't want to be thought unfit or stupid.*

"Most elegant! Beautiful work!" he announced.

So the tailors called for more money, more silk, and more gold thread. After a while, the emperor sent another statesman to check on the clothes that would soon be his. This man also praised the invisible robes for fear of being thought unfit or stupid.

Soon the day came when the emperor would march in a parade, showing off his new clothes. He arrived at the tailor shop with his courtiers, took off his old clothes, and donned the ones he could not see. Then the king marched naked through the town. No one wanted to admit he could see no clothes on the emperor. The chamberlains marching behind even held up a train of cloth that was not there. Thus, the emperor wore no clothes!

Only the Unfit or Stupid?

Our children face a similar challenge. People around them proclaim values that are not there and call what is clearly wrong "right" or at least "acceptable." Our kids are made to feel stupid and unfit if they don't join in recognizing "beauty" where ugliness actually exists.

When I walk across the lawn toward my daughters' middle school, open a magazine, watch TV, or listen to the radio, I am reminded time after time of the fierce battle we must wage for the lives and souls of our children. They're living in a world where sin jumps up and down in front of their faces, screaming, "If it feels good, do it!"

So what can we do to raise godly children in a world with no solid standards and unbiblical principles? Grab hold of the solid, unchanging hand of God, and teach His principles. Claiming God as my Husband becomes more than lip service when I uphold a principle and state with confidence to my children, "It's because your Father says so." When we show them the black-and-white truths of Scripture, we tell it the way it is and always will be, and what it means to them today. Here are some suggestions for how to help children stand strong, using Proverbs 7 as a framework. The passage is most directly a warning against prostitution, but it can apply to all moral hazards.

• **Be Wise and Discerning**

"At the window of my house I looked out through the lattice. I saw among the simple, I noticed among the young men, a youth who lacked judgment" (verses 6-7).

We must saturate our children with the truth of God's Word while they are under our care—through participation in church groups, family Bible studies, and other Christian influences in the home—so they will have the wisdom and discernment to recognize the difference between what's good and bad in our world, what's true and what's not.

Then also, just as we would close a window, secure a door, or plug a hole to prevent a draft from entering our home, we must do the same for the spiritual well-being of our families. Find the draft makers—TV, the telephone, non-Christian friends—and replace them with something better. Be creative about finding alternative activities, and be diligent about teaching God's principles for living. That's how our children learn sound judgment.

• Go to the Right Places

"He was going down the street near her corner, walking along in the direction of her house at twilight, as the day was fading, as the dark of night set in" (verses 8-9).

Our children must understand that as alluring as the enemy's territory may look, it's foolish and potentially catastrophic to go there. We must make them aware of the vastness of the territory he occupies in our fallen world. We must urge them to "enter through the narrow gate. For wide is the gate and broad is the road that leads to destruction, and many enter through it. But small is the gate and narrow the road that leads to life, and only a few find it" (Matthew 7:13-14).

• Listen to the Right Voices

"Then out came a woman to meet him, dressed like a prostitute and with crafty intent. (She is loud and defiant, her feet never stay at home)" (verses 10-11).

Not only must our children watch the places they go that make them vulnerable to the enemy's devices, but they must also be careful about the company they keep. The world is screaming, "Compromise!" We must help them learn how to turn a deaf ear to those who give wrong counsel, and we must show them the benefits of godly companions.

• Recognize Disguised Evil

"(Now in the street, now in the squares, at every corner she lurks.) She took hold of him and kissed him and with a brazen face she said: '. . . I looked for you and have found you! I have covered my beds with colored linens from Egypt. I have perfumed my bed with myrrh, aloes and cinnamon. Come, let's drink deep of love till morning; let's enjoy ourselves with love!'" (verses 12-18).

Sin has such a common face that it is sometimes hard to recognize it as sin. It can be enjoyable for a time—it looks good, smells good, and everyone is doing it. "Come on—no one will know," it says. Our kids begin to think theirs is the only house where Mom doesn't allow certain TV programs or Dad prohibits hanging out with the "in crowd." We must teach our children to see sin where it lurks and how insidious a stronghold it can establish in the weak, compromising, unprotected areas of their lives.

• Recognize the Power of Temptation

"With persuasive words she led him astray; she seduced him with her smooth talk" (verse 21).

Apart from Christ, no one is stronger than the temptation he or she confronts. But God assures us that "he will not let you be tempted beyond what you can bear. But when you are tempted, he will also provide a way out so that you can stand up under it" (1 Corinthians 10:13). Each child must cultivate his or her own relationship with Christ in order to recognize temptation and have the strength to say no.

• Remember the Consequences of Sin

"All at once he followed her like an ox going to the slaughter, like a deer stepping into a noose till an arrow pierces his liver, like a bird darting into a snare, little knowing it will cost him his life" (verses 22-23).

Death is the last consequence of sin. Sin is the consequence of yielding to temptation. Temptation is often the consequence of being in the wrong places and listening to the wrong voices. The pathway to destruction is simple, and a lot of people are on it. Don't let your children be among those who are.

"Now then, my sons, listen to me; pay attention to what I say. Do not let your heart turn to her ways or stray into her paths. Many are the victims she has brought down; her slain are a mighty throng. Her house is a highway to the grave, leading down to the chambers of death" (verses 24-27).

Victory Through Christ

When I get fearful about what could happen to my children, I become immobilized, trying to think how I can prevent it. Every time that happens, I remind myself of who I am in Christ. And when I do, I recall a lesson a pastor taught me regarding the power of the enemy.

This pastor was walking across the sands of the Arizona desert when he encountered a diamondback rattlesnake. He killed the snake and cut off its head. He was carrying the snake back to his truck when he realized that though dead, it was still shaking its rattle and lunging at him.

"What's more," the pastor said, "even though the snake's head was cut off, I continued to flinch."

We *and* our families must see that no matter how turbulent the world is, Satan's "head" was cut off at Calvary. He may continue to shake his rattle, but he has no power over us. We must teach our children to recognize and confront Satan's evil devices. We must impart courage to them to stand for what is right, no matter how many people tell them they are unfit or stupid. We must let them know that even if a million people stand for wrong, it is still wrong. And most of all, we must make them aware that in Christ, they are free, delivered from Satan's grasp.

The battle for our children must be waged first and foremost on our knees. Consider filling out the following commitment:

I will spend _____ minutes in prayer each day for my children. I will pray for _____, _____, and _____.

I will also increase my children's exposure to God's principles for living by _____, _____ and _____.

Date_____

Signature_____

"All your sons will be taught by the Lord, and great will be your children's peace" (Isaiah 54:13).

10

Encouragement for the Down Times

One warm Ohio summer afternoon when I was in my early twenties, I spread a blanket in my backyard to enjoy the brilliance of the sun. Fluffing the pillow and situating myself with a cold drink and a novel, I looked forward to getting lost in a romance.

Exhaustion soon overtook me from the events of the week before. First I had gotten word of an additional class I would be teaching in the fall, which would demand intense preparation during the weeks before school began. Then I had broken off a four-year relationship with a man who had meant a lot to me. Finally, I had bought my first house and now faced the demands of monthly payments and maintenance.

My skin was warm as I sipped at my drink and sighed with relief that the week was over. I opened my book to begin the first chapter when suddenly, without warning, I had an unexpected visitor. A big, black bird dipped low from the branch of a nearby tree and excreted right in my face.

Plop!

I still remember my hurried trip to the house to wash the mess from my face as I prayed, "God, why me?" And that's still my cry after more than a decade of dealing with the single-parent dailies, like getting up at the crack of dawn to peel onions for the crockpot; solving crises at work; deciding which bills will wait for next month; meeting with a child's teacher; "helping" my daughter solve math problems when I don't even know how to pronounce the name of the theorem she's studying.

Then on top of the ordinary, I receive calls that inform me I have to return to court, or a family member has grown ill, or I'll need to come up with $500 extra by the end of the month.

When these things happen, I need to pull back and remember that I am still a child of God. People like Balaam help me to do that.

The Man Who Carried the Message

Balaam's story is found in Numbers 22–24. The king of Moab was worried that his kingdom would be the next to fall to the invading Israelites. So he sent his men bearing great riches across many miles to convince soothsayer Balaam to curse the Israelites. Balaam had a reputation for being able to bring curses or blessings with his spoken word.

At last the king's men arrived back in Moab with Balaam in tow. The next morning, the king took Balaam atop a high mountain where he could see the great numbers of Israelites camped in the valley below. Balaam asked to have seven altars built and seven bulls and rams prepared for sacrifice. Then he went off and heard from God about whether he should curse Israel.

Balaam came back and told the king of Moab, "How can I curse those whom God has not cursed? How can I denounce those whom the Lord has not denounced? . . . Who can count the dust of Jacob or number the fourth part of Israel? Let me die the death of the righteous, and may my end be like theirs!" (Numbers 23:8, 10).

Not surprisingly, that was not what the king wanted to hear. He was frustrated and said, "What have you done to me? I brought you to curse my enemies, but you have done nothing but bless them!" Then he took Balaam to a second mountain where he could see only a part of the vast numbers of Israelites.

Again the altars were built, and again Balaam went to talk with God.

He returned with these words: "God is not a man, that he should lie, nor a son of man, that he should change his mind. Does he speak and then not act? Does he promise and not fulfill? I have received a command to bless; he has blessed, and I cannot change it" (Numbers 23:19-20).

The king was nothing if not persistent. He took Balaam to a *third* mountain and asked him once again to curse Israel. The altars were built, and God gave Balaam these words to deliver: "How beautiful are your tents, O Jacob, your dwelling places, O Israel! Like valleys they spread out, like gardens beside a river, like aloes planted by the Lord, like cedars beside the waters. Water will flow from their buckets; their seed will have abundant water" (Numbers 24:5-7).

In other words, the people of Israel were God's chosen ones, and He was going to bless them no matter what their enemies might desire or devise. As His people today, we, too, are recipients of His blessing and under His watchful care.

Good Now As Then

When my children were toddlers, they had a bear toy I called Weeble Wobble that was weighted on the bottom. The kids would punch and kick at him mercilessly. The bear would fall over countless times each day, then always roll back up again.

When I became a single mom, I wasn't resilient. Life had been pretty cushy for me, and someone was always there to help me through the difficulties. But parenting on my own brought (and still brings) many opportunities to bounce back. I also listen to incredible single-parent stories from across the country that make me wonder how any human being can endure so much.

But then I see those same moms and dads smile, or I hear the calmness return to their voices, as they recall the ways that God has come through for them. During those times, I imagine a room filled with all kinds of

Weeble Wobbles from across the world. As I see them roll back onto their feet, again and again, God is proved faithful.

And somewhere in the background of that room, I hear the same voice that Balaam heard saying, "You must not put a curse on these people, because they are blessed" and "Like valleys they spread out, like gardens beside a river, like aloes planted by the Lord, like cedars beside the waters. Water will flow from their buckets; their seed will have abundant water."

That's promise enough to Weeble-Wobble us and our children through anything!

❈ ❈ ❈ ❈ ❈ ❈ ❈ ❈

1. List the ways you have been "punched" or "kicked" during this past week.

2. Which of those difficulties seems too big for God to handle?

3. Commit the verse below to memory. Then at those times when you feel down, let the words roll you back up again.

"They may curse, but you will bless; when they attack they will be put to shame" (Psalm 109:28).

11

Through His Eyes

The old rocker creaked in rhythm with the breathing of my tiny, sleeping son. I rested my head against the back of the chair in one of those rare moments of quiet while the older children also snuggled in afternoon slumber.

I stroked my son's hair and sighed as I felt the burden of my daily life. *Every day, every need of the family falls squarely into my lap,* I thought. *What does the future hold? It's not fair that I get no help from my husband. How can such a man deserve to live?*

My thoughts were interrupted by the giggles of two little girls bumping on their bottoms down the steps, fresh and ready to go again. I smiled at the sound in spite of myself and returned the two hugs that soon greeted me.

My rest ended, I went to the kitchen to prepare the evening meal. I laid out the coloring book and crayons to occupy the girls as I began peeling potatoes. A phone call interrupted the peeling, then the pealing laughter of the girls interrupted the call. I settled a fuss, prepared the meat, and folded two loads of laundry.

With dinner ready, we gathered around the table. A brief moment of silence came during the prayer; then questions and laughter followed. Everyone spoke at once.

Dinner was almost finished when Ashley looked pensively out the window and got that questioning look in her eyes. "Mommy, why does the bird's nest upstairs on the light have only the mommy to take care of the babies?" she asked. "You never see the daddy. But the one in the front yard has both a mommy and a daddy to take care of the family."

The innocent words of the child renewed the spark of resentment in me, and the flame began to burn once again. *Yes,* I thought, *why doesn't she have any help?*

I wiped the children's faces, cleaned the table, then went outside and helped them gather toys before a spring thunderstorm arrived. I pulled my hair from my eyes, then chased a ball that the wind had blown across the yard.

We hurried back inside as the rain began to fall. I read their favorite book, though the words were nearly memorized. The girls kissed their baby brother and patted his head, then crawled across the back of the couch to get a better view of the pictures.

Suddenly, the lights went out with a crash of thunder. The girls clutched at my skirt for security and helped me find a candle. Their giggles and happy conversation followed the glow of the candle up the stairs. They tried to blow out the flame. I finally got them into their beds and, at last, all three succumbed to sleep.

After kissing them good night and tucking in their blankets, I walked wearily into my room and lay across the bed. I listened as the rain, beating down in torrents, changed to hail. A gust of wind blew some branches against the side of the house, and the nest resting above the light on the balcony outside my bedroom door fell to the floor below.

Three baby birds groped for protection. They were hungry, cold, and frightened. Hail pelted them as the mother bird flew to the railing a few feet away, cowering against the wind.

I watched and waited in the darkness for the mother to come back to her young ones. When the hail began again, I reached outside and pulled the nest and trembling babies under a lawn chair beside the door. The mother remained distant, shivering in the cold.

Suddenly, memories of my long day and thoughts of the morrow overwhelmed me. Hot tears of questions, frustrations, and exhaustion poured out. "Why, God?" I prayed. "Isn't it enough that I must raise my three children alone? Do I also have to save these three birds tonight? Where are You? Where is my husband?"

The electricity had returned by now. I walked to the side of my bed and turned on the light. Angrily, I picked up my Bible. It fell open, and I read, "He who is full loathes the honey, but to the hungry even what is bitter tastes sweet. Like a bird that strays from its nest is a man who strays from his home" (Proverbs 27:7-8).

I stretched back and thought about the words I had read. I thought of my husband's searching and unhappy eyes and of his wandering to fill his hungry soul. Then I prayed:

"Oh, God, forgive me. Help me to see him through Your eyes, and remove the bitterness from my heart. Help me to take the responsibilities You have given me to shelter, feed, protect, and teach my children with a smile on my lips and joy in my heart."

I went into the bathroom and washed the tears from my eyes—somehow feeling lighter. Then I walked to my bedroom door and peered outside, where only the distant lightning remained from the storm. My gaze shifted to the ground, where the mother bird was now feeding three hungry little ones and snuggling down to comfort them.

The clock said 4:00 A.M. I sighed, my task accomplished, my day finally done. In a few hours, my own babies would awaken with little chirps, and I must respond. But somehow I knew the strength would be there, as long as I kept my eyes on Christ and saw things through His eyes.

I closed my eyes with a smile on my face and joy in my heart.

※ ※ ※ ※ ※ ※ ※ ※

Sit quietly before the Lord, and allow Him to minister to your spirit. Ask Him to change the ways you have looked at the one who hurt you. Our afflictions are for the present, but the saving of a soul is for eternity, long after all indiscretions are forgotten.

Be specific. Pray for the exact needs in that person's life. Then ask God to help you see everyone and every situation through His eyes.

"But you, O God, are my king from of old; you bring salvation upon the earth" (Psalm 74:12).

12

The Chosen One

"I choose Johnny."

"I choose Kathy."

I can still remember, as a child at school, standing in line to be chosen for a baseball team—the anticipation, the fear, the excitement. *I'm a really good pitcher—but what if they don't think so? What if neither of them wants me and I'm left standing while the others take the field?*

Well, I was never more proud than the day I was finally the first to be picked. Somebody thought I was the best pitcher on the playground!

Many years later, I found myself once again in a lineup, this time unwelcomed. Suddenly I was chosen to be a single mother of three. *I don't* want *to do this alone,* I wailed night after night. I didn't go anywhere or do anything but feel sorry for myself and the terrible deal I had been handed. I sat inside my misery, looking at a future that seemed to hold only darkness, despair, and defeat.

One day, my thoughts of doom were disrupted by the giggles of two little girls and my tiny infant son, who was trying to roll over for the first time. The call had been sounded. I realized life was going on whether I liked the forecast or not. Three children had lives to live—tricycles to ride, balls to hit, and books to read. God was calling me to stand up and accept the job I had been chosen for and to do so with strength and courage.

I rose from my place of weakness and walked uncertainly to my team. I gathered the players, and we took the field. Unlike my childhood days, now there were many positions I needed to play. I had to pitch the right things to my children and intercept the bad while running with all the speed I could muster to cover the bases. Most of the time, it seemed there were countless balls in the air at the same time. But if I ever stopped, so would the game, and the team would disband.

The game locations have changed, the challenges have varied, and the weather has not always cooperated. But we're still a team, and God has chosen me to be the captain. During those earlier games, the skills were learned, the qualities were cultivated, and the commands were received that caused the victories to take place—one game at a time.

While some games have been close calls, and a few have been lost, this captain moves on to the next game with confidence, knowing that my sufficiency is from the Lord—my Manager. The One who *chose* me in the first place is teaching me more skills all the time, and my one goal is to play my best for Him.

Open your Bible and notice those whom God called.

Hebrews 11:8-10 and 13-16, for example, tells how Abraham was one of those honored for his strong faith in the Lord. He, too, was *chosen* by God to do a special job. By looking at his example, we can gain insight into our own journeys with the Lord.

✄　✄　✄　✄　✄　✄　✄　✄

1. Read verse 8. When God called Abraham to go forward in what He had for him to do, Abraham obeyed. How much did he know about where he was going or what those tasks would demand?

When you were chosen by the Lord to become a single parent, did you know what all that involved? How did you proceed from that point? Describe some of the tasks along the way and how God proved His faithfulness. (Also see Isaiah 45:2.)

2. Read verse 9. What kinds of people did Abraham meet on his journey? Why was that important?

What kinds of people have been most helpful or harmful in supporting and assisting you?

3. Read verse 10. On what did Abraham set his sights that sustained him through rigorous challenges?

Have your situations and needs for reliance on God changed your sights or priorities in any way? What is most important to you now?

4. The first verse of Hebrews 11 says, "Faith is being sure of what we hope for and certain of what we do not see." Now read verse 13. How was faith for the needs of Abraham and others cultivated before they ever received the promise?

Describe ways your faith has grown through your single-parenting challenges.

5. Read verse 15. Why was it necessary for Abraham and the others to leave and forget what was behind them in order to move forward?

Philippians 3:12 says, "Forgetting what is behind and straining toward what is ahead, I press on toward the goal to win the prize for which God has called me heavenward in Christ Jesus." What do you need to forget?

6. How can you know which way to go and what decisions to make? Read Isaiah 48:17. Set aside a specific time each day in which you can talk to God and allow Him to lead you.

Be strong! You have been chosen.

"Consider now, for the Lord has chosen you to build a temple as a sanctuary. Be strong and do the work" (1 Chronicles 28:10).

13

Pines from the Thorns

Not long after my divorce and return to Christ, I gathered the remains of my shattered dreams to move forward with life. From every angle, I looked at what my children and I had been through and saw no way things would turn out okay.

Then I found a verse in the Bible: "Instead of the thornbush will grow the pine tree, and instead of briers the myrtle will grow. This will be for the Lord's renown, for an everlasting sign, which will not be destroyed" (Isaiah 55:13).

Finding that verse changed the way I prayed. I called it my "lemonade from lemons" verse as I asked God to take care of circumstances surrounding our lives. I asked God to be faithful to bring about something good in my family in spite of what had gone wrong.

Two years later, I bought our first home in Ohio. I fixed it up with wallpaper, paint, and decorations. I cleaned out the yard, and then I called a landscape artist to help me do something with a problem spot where water stood after rain and killed the plants.

He came to our home and carefully examined the damp conditions, sun exposure, and soil consistency. Then he left and came back with new soil, seeds, bulbs, and plants. He built up the land and carefully placed the plants he had selected especially for our conditions.

The next spring, brilliant iris and crocus peaked through, and hemlock trees and pussy willows flourished in the standing puddles left by the spring showers. As I picked the tender red strawberries from plants that covered the mounds around the trees, I was amazed at how someone could grow something so beautiful in a place that had produced so little of value before.

Each spring thereafter, I measured the growth of the hemlocks and cut new pussy willow branches for bouquets. I also continued to measure the growth God had brought about in our single-parent home. I pondered the once-bleak future and the adverse effects divorce was supposed to bring upon my children. I realized that the day I chose to give my life to God, my problem spots became His. I have, in turn, watched Him create a happy home led by one very thankful mom.

While Waiting

To keep that new garden growing, I had to remain busy. I weeded, fertilized, and sprayed against intruders throughout the long, hot summers. Similarly, I discovered that if God was at work, bringing about something good in my life, there were things I must do while I waited.

In Jeremiah 29, I found instruction about what to do during life's holding patterns. The passage contains a letter Jeremiah wrote to the Israelites who had been taken into Babylonian captivity. They were going to remain captive for 70 years. And though they didn't want to be there, God had specific things He wanted them to do while they waited.

• "Build houses and settle down; plant gardens and eat what they produce" (verse 5).

After my divorce, I wanted to do nothing but feel sorry for myself. But that day my infant son rolled over for the first time, I realized life was going on with or without me. My kids had the right to get on with the thrilling business of living. I had the responsibility to help them do that.

God wants us to make homes. The cookies and laughter, and even the tough times, are things from which memories are built.

• "Marry and have sons and daughters; find wives for your sons and give your daughters in marriage, so that they too may have sons and daughters. Increase in number there; do not decrease" (verse 6).

As single parents, we can easily forget the importance of helping our kids develop normal relationships with members of the opposite sex. The task becomes difficult when one parent is not there to share the load and the children aren't able to see a solid husband-wife relationship modeled every day.

God commands us to grow our children with firm teaching in the faith, giving them specific criteria for relationships. To raise them as normal, fruitful Christians who marry more of the same, we need a specific strategy, along with our consistent prayers for them *and* their future mates. This is God's plan, and He will help us carry it out.

• "Seek the peace and prosperity of the city to which I have carried you into exile" (verse 7).

Many of us came to single parenting through treachery and deceit by a spouse we trusted. When we refuse to forgive that spouse—the one who "carried us into exile"—we hurt ourselves and our children, and we prevent our lives from moving forward the way God wants.

Through God's grace, we *are* able to forgive those who have hurt us. Though we may never be close again, memories of the past do not have to impede our present.

• "Do not let the prophets and diviners among you deceive you" (verse 8).

When an absence is created in our lives, we sometimes have the urge to fill that void with anything that comes along, and the quicker the better. God cautions us to know the Word and have a solid relationship with the Father so we can have a discerning eye and tell the truth from the lie.

As we remain obedient to Christ, He is free to move in our lives and bring about good from the bad that has happened. Our relationship with Him also prevents us from making future wrong decisions. Meanwhile, He has the opportunity to grow us into the people He wants us to be.

So what can we expect when this time of "captivity" is over?

• "When seventy years are completed for Babylon, I will come to you and fulfill my gracious promise to bring you back to this place. For I know the plans I have for you" (verses 10-11).

When I was a child and my parents promised me something, I knew they would do what they told me, though sometimes the fulfillment was delayed.

In these verses, your Father promises that when the difficult waiting-and-growing time has passed, you will be okay. He has known you all along. He has carefully studied your situation, and no matter what He has to work with, He has plans for you.

Look for the Good

Sometimes when we gaze into the dark places of our lives where plants have withered and died, we say, "There's no hope for what is presently growing there, nor for anything else of value to grow in its place." But when we find those barren spots, we have choices: We can struggle and ultimately accept what comes out of those tragedies; we can fret and stew but do nothing; or we can surrender our problem spots to the Master Landscaper and be obedient in doing our part to help the new growth.

Only God knows how to take flower beds of tragedy and sorrow and turn them into lush gardens. Only He knows what to plant no matter what grew there before and no matter what happened to destroy it. Only He knows how to fertilize, nourish, and even add new dimensions. Only He knows us and our children by name and the number of hairs on our heads.

Only God holds the pieces to the master plan. And when these circumstances are handed to Him, only He has the ability to bring joy from sorrow, good from bad, and a myrtle tree from briers.

❈ ❈ ❈ ❈ ❈ ❈ ❈ ❈

1. Which of your problem spots has God already fixed?

2. What else do you need God to do?

3. Though you can't change your circumstances, is there more you can do while you wait?

4. Memorize God's promise below that everything is going to be okay.

"And we know that in all things God works for the good of those who love him, who have been called according to his purpose" (Romans 8:28).

14

A Roaring Lion

Lucifer the lion (see 1 Peter 5:8) moved quietly, deliberately through the streets, marking his territory. His ravenous appetite controlled his every move. He drooled as he remembered his last tasty meal—a victim caught unaware. He had moved in behind him from an unexpected place, then pounced. The less they knew of his plans, the easier Lucifer's job became. His hunger drove him mercilessly toward his goal—to kill and steal and destroy.

Two other lions who took their orders from Lucifer, Mersed and Nod, walked close by. They were smaller and weaker, but they were Lucifer's pride and joy.

"I think we shall take young and tender ones today. 'Teens,' they call them," Lucifer said. "They make satisfying meals and are so easy to seduce these days."

The Preoccupied

Soon they came to a neighborhood where lawns were neatly clipped and wreaths hung on the front doors. Lucifer decided it was a perfect place for devastation. They waited on a side street to scout it out. Which of the houses could they enter?

Before long, two boys came walking down the street. They smoked cigarettes and yelled profanities. "Some of our own," Lucifer said. "They will help." The boys stopped at the house on the corner.

"Jeffrey!" they yelled through an open window. "Open the door and let us in!"

Before long, a face appeared. Jeffrey smiled and said, "I'll be right there."

Lucifer and his pride had their chance to slip in. The door opened wide, and they were inside. Lucifer's mouth watered as he walked toward their unsuspecting victim. The boys slipped Jeffrey a cigarette as they all moved quickly to the basement.

"This one is yours," Lucifer told Mersed, the smaller lion. "Much too easy a challenge for me."

Mersed moved greedily down the steps behind the boys.

Lucifer and Nod walked to the kitchen. A large calendar that was fully marked occupied a wall, and a note lay on the counter that read: "Jeffrey: Your dad is working late. I have a meeting until 9:00 at the women's club. Eat the leftovers in the fridge, and we'll see you when we get home. Mom."

Lucifer smiled and said, "Our work here will be well underway before anyone is home."

Lucifer and Nod walked back outside. They took their place once again at the corner and watched for their next victim.

The Sleeper

Soon the streets were full of passing cars coming home from work. Lucifer and Nod were growing hungrier. One car nearly ran them down. It made Lucifer growl quietly in anger. "Let's follow that one," he commanded.

The car turned into a driveway not far away. A father jumped out to move a bicycle from his pathway and mumbled something under his breath, then pulled the car into the garage. His loosened tie blew across his shoulder as he walked to the mailbox.

The man moved toward the house. He stuck his key in the door and opened it wide. Lucifer and Nod slid through.

The man hardly said a word as he brushed by his wife in the kitchen. Lucifer spotted the daughter through an opening in her bedroom door. She sat on her bed, wearing earphones and tapping her pencil on the book that lay in front of her. She was unaware that Dad was home. She was unaware of almost everything.

A short time later, dinner was over, and so was the little bit of conversation. The family members moved their silent ways to separate parts of the house. Mom cleaned up the kitchen. Daughter went back to her bedroom. Dad stole to his study with the newspaper and the adult-only videotape he had hidden in his briefcase.

Two hours passed. Eyes grew heavy. Dad and Mom mumbled good night to their daughter, who responded, "Yeah, whatever." And they walked toward their bedroom for the night.

The house was quiet. Lucifer and Nod decided it was time to go in for the kill. The daughter rose from her bed. She walked to Dad's study and found the tape he had brought home. She looked over her shoulder, pulled the joint she had gotten at school from her pocket, and closed the door. But not before Nod entered. "This one's mine," he muttered.

While Mom and Dad slept peacefully upstairs, Lucifer smiled and walked back out the door. Mission accomplished. Now it was his turn.

The Wise

Lucifer moved with stealth down the street. He tried several doors, but he couldn't get in. He searched for an opening most of the night. As the morning dawned, he stopped. He would take the house where he stood. He was tired and hungry. He would look no further.

Up he walked toward the door. It was fastened, but Lucifer heard a woman's voice coming through an open window beside the front porch. He was startled. It was early dawn—usually the best time of all to catch people sleeping and unaware.

Lucifer tried to roar. Only a hoarse whisper came out.

"I will replace the lies I have believed," the woman continued, "with truths such as, 'In all these things we are more than conquerors through him who loved us' (Romans 8:37). And instead of ever believing those lies again, I will believe Your Word that never, ever changes. Thank You, God, for saving my family."

Lucifer cowered in the corner. He reached for the woman, but his strength failed.

From a single-parent home in the neighborhood with neatly clipped lawns and wreaths on the doors, a song could be heard coming through the open window. The lion, Lucifer, could not be seen slinking out through that same window. But he was, as fast as he could go. He could not return as long as the woman continued to resist him in the power of the Lord. He had no place. She was more than a conqueror.

The Bible tells us that many of our battles can be won only with spiritual weapons through prayer (see 2 Corinthians 10:4). To help equip yourself for that spiritual conflict, memorize the following Scriptures, and take the corresponding steps to victory.

- **Repent.**
Conviction is the work of the Holy Spirit. "If we confess our sins, he is faithful and just to forgive us our sins and to cleanse us from all unrighteousness" (1 John 1:9).

- **Refuse to let things go any further.**
When you willingly go down paths you know you shouldn't, you give Satan permission to attack with destructive thoughts and temptations. "In order that Satan might not outwit us. For we are not unaware of his schemes" (2 Corinthians 2:11).

Lucifer's curiosity drew him nearer. He rested his ear against the window screen.

"God," he heard, "I am so alone since the children's father left. Things are really hard. Monica is 14, and she's being tempted with things I don't think she can overcome. This one's too big to handle. There's no way out. . . . " The woman's voice drifted off.

The words made Lucifer's ears ache. He dipped his head and rubbed against his shoulder. When the talk ceased, so did his pain. The woman cried.

Lucifer pulled the screen back far enough to climb through the big window. Boldly he sat on the floor to plan his strategy.

The woman picked up the Bible that lay beside her on the couch. Her voice was shaky as she began to read out loud: "Be self-controlled and alert. Your enemy the devil prowls around like a roaring lion looking for someone to devour" (1 Peter 5:8).

The woman wiped her eyes and straightened her back. She read on. "The thief comes only to steal and kill and destroy; I have come that they may have life, and have it to the full" (John 10:10).

The woman looked up and repeated, "I have come that they may have life to the full?" She pondered the words, then went on.

"Dear God. I don't have to accept defeat on my daughter's behalf. Forgive me for thinking I did."

Lucifer moved uncomfortably.

"I take back the ground in my home that I have surrendered to the devil. You cannot have my daughter, Satan. You cannot have my home."

This is not good. Lucifer thought. *I will have to show my strength.* He moved in closer to the woman, but he could not reach her. He strained, but she continued.

"Please make my mind to know that nothing is impossible with You. Help me to remember always that greater is He that is in me than he that is in the world" (1 John 4:4).

- **Resist the lies of Satan.**

The fortress of lies Satan builds in your heart and mind can't be destroyed by weapons of flesh. "The weapons we fight with are not the weapons of the world. On the contrary, they have divine power to demolish strongholds" (2 Corinthians 10:4).

- **Believe the truth**

Replace Satan's lies with a tower of truth. This means reprogramming your mind with truth about yourself, God, and Satan (see Romans 12:2). When the enemy comes at you with intruding thoughts, flee to the tower. "The name of the Lord is a strong tower. The righteous run to it and are safe" (Proverbs 18:10).

- **Control your thoughts.**

The mind is the primary battleground between God and Satan in spiritual warfare. "We demolish arguments and every pretension that sets itself up against the knowledge of God, and we take captive every thought to make it obedient to Christ" (2 Corinthians 10:5).

"Submit yourselves, then, to God. Resist the devil, and he will flee from you. Come near to God and he will come near to you" (James 4:7-8).

15

Move Along

One of the many emotions I felt after my husband left was humiliation—in the grocery store, at church, at my daughter's preschool. I wanted to buy an ad in the newspaper, announce in the local churches, and call everyone I knew to prove I had been a good wife, mother, and daughter-in-law.

One night as I was talking to God about the injustices I had endured, He seemed to say, "You've done all you can. Move on with your life, and don't stay behind trying to prove anything to others. Those who matter already know."

The Example of Christ

One thing we quickly learn as Christians is that bad things continue to happen. We get sick. We lose loved ones. But we have the assurance that we experience nothing that Christ did not also go through (see Hebrews 4:15).

It's common, for example, to be treated unfairly. Here's what the Bible says about it: "But how is it to your credit if you receive a beating for doing wrong and endure it? But if you suffer for doing good and you endure it, this is commendable before God. To this you were called, because Christ suffered for you, leaving you an example, that you should follow in his steps" (1 Peter 2:20-21). So what was Christ's example?

"He committed no sin" (1 Peter 2:22). You and I will never attain that level of perfection. But we are called to holy living in the power of the Holy Spirit (see Galatians 5:16-25). This involves staying in God's Word so we know how we should think and act. It also means spending consistent time in prayer, asking for forgiveness for mistakes and seeking direction for what's to come. It means having fellowship with other believers, through church, friends, and family, who can hold us accountable for how we live.

"No deceit was found in his mouth" (1 Peter 2:22). You and I are not to represent anything but truth—no lying, cheating, or manipulating in any way. This can be difficult if someone is waiting to destroy us for the slightest real or imagined mistake. Nothing short of daily prayer is sufficient, asking God for His wisdom in all we say and do. We can also pray that God will change the heart of the people who hurt us.

"When they hurled their insults at him, he did not retaliate" (1 Peter 2:23). God instructs us to give up our desire to get even. This was the hardest task of all for me as I imagined the terrible things that I wanted to haunt my former husband. But in order to move on and receive healing, we must release vengeance to God. This can happen only as we open ourselves up in prayer.

"When he suffered, he made no threats. Instead, he entrusted himself to him who judges justly" (1 Peter 2:23). Sometimes, saying nothing is the most spiritual thing we can do. "Teach me, and I will be quiet; show me where I have been wrong" (Job 6:24). "The quiet words of the wise are more to be heeded than the shouts of a ruler of fools" (Ecclesiastes 9:17). Be still, and let God do His best work.

Others Who Were Abused

Another man in the Bible who knew the pain of being treated unfairly was Joseph. His story is found in Genesis 37–50.

You'll recall from an earlier devotional in this book that because

Joseph was his father's favorite, his other brothers became jealous. So they sold him into slavery in Egypt. And even there, he was thrown into prison because of a false accusation made against him. Individuals he helped while in prison promptly forgot him when they had the opportunity to assist him in return.

What had Joseph done to deserve any of this treatment? His life was marked by faithfulness to God. Though he had reason to be disturbed over the injustices, not a single bitter word by him is recorded in Scripture. His faith in God was immovable, even when he didn't understand what was going on. He committed no sin in regard to his unfair treatment. No deceit was found in his mouth. He did not retaliate. He made no threats, but entrusted himself to God's judgment.

Time Proven

Recently I received a letter that showed me I've made at least some progress in this area. It was from a pastor who had heard me do a radio interview. He has known me for a long time but had not seen or been in contact with me in quite a while, and he was kind enough to say that he believed I had grown in the Lord in the interim.

That pastor was the minister of the first church I attended with my husband and his family, and he knew what we had gone through. I couldn't help but remember the lesson God began teaching me more than a decade before: *Don't stay behind trying to prove anything to others. Those who matter already know.* This pastor was one who knew.

❧ ❧ ❧ ❧ ❧ ❧ ❧ ❧

What about you? Moving forward begins with taking one step at a time in the right direction, with God's help. The questions below can help you determine what your first steps might need to be:

• What has happened to you that you did not deserve?

• Who hurt you?

• Have you asked God to forgive your own sins?

• Do you try to live each day and make every decision as Christ would?

• How can you improve in this area of your life?

• Do you measure everything you say with truth and discretion? Incorporate Psalm 19:14 into your prayers: "May the words of my mouth and the meditation of my heart be pleasing in your sight."

• What situations challenge you most in recognizing and upholding the truth? Name ways you can avoid these circumstances.

• Have you given up your desire to get even? If not, you remain locked in a prison of your own making, which will keep you from moving forward.

• Proverbs 25:21-22 says, "If your enemy is hungry, give him food to eat; if he is thirsty, give him water to drink. In doing this, you will heap burning coals on his head." The last part of that verse refers to a Middle Eastern act of kindness in which someone gives hot coals from his fire to another, who carries them home in a head-borne container to restart his own fire.

What does this mean in your circumstances? What can you do to "heap burning coals" on the head of the one who hurt you?

"Do not repay evil with evil or insult with insult, but with blessing, because to this you were called so that you may inherit a blessing" (1 Peter 3:9).

16

Did God Know?

One day, I returned home from a business trip. I walked past the airport baggage claim area to the parking lot to get my car first, thinking I could save some time and get away sooner once the luggage came.

I pulled the car to the curb, ran into the airport, and grabbed my garment bag and suitcase. I was back out in less than four minutes. But where was my car?

I asked a policeman who stood nearby, and he replied, "It was just towed. If you had had someone to stay in the car, you would have been okay."

Hot tears stung my eyes as I dragged my luggage past my first parking space to the lot where the towed cars were kept. I paid my $60 grudgingly as I muttered under my breath, "But I don't *have* someone to stay with my car! I don't have anyone but me. Does God even know about all the hassles I have to endure?"

Today in the United States, more than 10 million homes are headed by single parents. The numbers are greater than they've ever been, but are the problems? How much of what we struggle with is specific to the times in which we live? Are we a forgotten group who doesn't really fit anywhere?

The Bible refers to widows and orphans more than 50 times. It's filled with stories about real people who struggled with the kinds of issues we face today—including a widow and a divorcée. With all the things they went through, did God know?

The Widowed

The city was Zarephath on the Mediterranean coast of Phoenicia. A widow was gathering sticks by the town gate one day. Life had been hard since she lost her husband. She and her son were down to their last handful of flour and a little oil in the bottom of a jug. With a heavy heart, the woman was collecting firewood to bake their last meal as she prepared for them to die.

Then up walked a man—a prophet called Elijah—and from the moment she saw him, her life was forever changed. "Would you bring me a little water in a jar so I may have a drink?" he asked her. As she was going to get it, he called, "And bring me, please, a piece of bread" (1 Kings 17:10-11).

Oh, great, the woman must have thought. *I don't have anything to feed my son and me, let alone someone else. But what's one more mouth and one less meal?*

Elijah said to her, however, "Don't be afraid. Go home and do as you have said. But first make a small cake of bread for me from what you have and bring it to me, and then make something for yourself and your son. For this is what the Lord, the God of Israel, says: 'The jar of flour will not be used up and the jug of oil will not run dry until the day the Lord gives rain on the land'" (1 Kings 17:13-14).

The widow went away and did what Elijah asked. The next morning, she was amazed to find more flour and oil remained—and the day after and the day after. God had not promised her jars would always be full but that they would never run dry. And that's just what happened.

Time went by, and the food was always there. But then the woman's son grew ill and eventually died. Because single women in Phoenicia could not earn a living except as prostitutes or slaves, a widow could only hope to scrape by until her sons were old enough to support her in her old age. So now this widow stood especially bereaved—without a husband, without her son, and without hope for the future.

I just knew this was too good to be true. I have my cakes, but now I don't have my son. God has truly forgotten me now.

"What do you have against me?" she asked Elijah. "Did you come to remind me of my sin and kill my son?" (1 Kings 17:18).

But Elijah carried the woman's son up to the room where he was staying and prayed for him. God answered that prayer for the widow He loved, returning the boy's life to him. Elijah carried the boy to his mother and said, "Look, your son is alive!" (1 Kings 17:22).

Did God know this woman who was poor, needy, and alone? He not only knew her, but He used her in ministry to others as well. Did God make provisions for her? Yes, and not just for that day but for all the days and challenges to come. Did God know about the sins she had committed in the past, and was He punishing her for them in the death of her son? No, God had not only forgiven her sins because of her faith, but He had also forgotten them and was moving on with new plans for her life.

The Divorced

The place? Canaan. Hagar was a single mom we read about in Genesis, beginning in chapter 15. She was a slave from Egypt, probably a gift from Pharaoh to a wealthy man named Abram (see Genesis 12:16). Hagar worked for his wife, Sarai.

God had promised Abram and Sarai a son to carry on the family name (see 15:4). But after years of waiting, it seemed apparent to Sarai that God helps those who help themselves. She was certain she was too old to have children, so there was only one thing to do: help God out! Sarai knew that in their society, a barren wife could provide her husband with her personal handmaiden to bear a child in her place. So

Sarai offered Hagar to bear Abram a son that Sarai could adopt, and Abram consented (see 16:2).

A few years after Hagar had given birth to Ishmael, Sarah (her new name) gave birth to Isaac by miraculous means. According to ancient custom, if a man accepted the son of a slave woman as his own child, that son would receive part of the man's inheritance. If he were the man's first son, he would receive the largest portion of the inheritance. But the father could choose instead not to acknowledge that slave child as his heir. He could free the slave child and his mother and send them away. If Hagar and Ishmael stayed, then, Isaac could not receive the full inheritance, so Sarah insisted that they be freed and sent away.

Abraham (his new name) sent Hagar away with some provisions, though not enough for her to reach one of the desert settlements that existed in those days (see 21:14-15). Hagar was essentially like a divorcée, though she had never formally married Abraham.

When Abraham's provisions ran out, God's kicked in. As Hagar sat under a tree, unable to watch her son die, "God heard the boy crying, and the angel of God called to her from heaven and said to her, 'What is the matter, Hagar?'" (21:17).

She had been rejected by the closest thing she had to a husband, and she felt utterly destitute. Abraham had not provided enough child support to make it through the desert, but God had. When Hagar felt the most alone and thought they would both perish, God intervened with miraculous provision: "'Lift the boy up and take him by the hand, for I will make him into a great nation.' Then God opened her eyes and she saw a well of water. So she went and filled the skin with water and gave the boy a drink" (21:18-19).

Did God know Hagar and her son? You bet. Did God make provision as the boy grew? "God was with the boy as he grew up" (21:20).

He Knew

To the poor, needy, lonely widow, God gave provisions that never ran out. Though she was an outsider, He made her an integral part of His plan. God also reached out to an unknown single mom in the desert, called her by name, and took her fatherless son and made him a great nation.

Does He know what you and I are going through? He knows. No matter what the place or time you are in, God knows.

Tell Him what you are going through. He knows, but He wants to hear from you. Tell Him exactly what you need.

❧ ❧ ❧ ❧ ❧ ❧ ❧ ❧

The Bible says in James 4:2, "You do not have, because you do not ask God."

1. What emotional areas are you struggling with?

2. Where would you like for God to help you in your parenting?

3. When do you struggle most with adult issues?

4. How could you use His help financially?

5. Tell God what you're going through. He knows, but He wants to hear from you.

"But he knows the way I take; when he has tested me, I will come forth as gold" (Job 23:10).

17

Singularly Significant

Most single parents come to singleness kicking and screaming. But child-rearing issues are often not the ones that cause the most concern. Rather, many individuals worry about spending the rest of their lives alone.

A man cries out to God in the morning to bring him a wife. A woman pleads for someone to be a father to her child. Then when the prayer is over, they fret and fume throughout the day. Loneliness clouds their ability to perform the tasks God has called them to do.

My dad was a postman when I was a child. During the cold Ohio winters, since his car was parked outside, he would put a piece of cardboard over his windshield at night to keep his visibility clear the next morning. As soon as he went out with his steaming cup of coffee, he would start the car and carefully remove the cardboard. Then he would back down the driveway and go about his day.

I often think of this when I hear single parents talk of their preoccupation with finding a mate. My dad never could have moved forward if he had not first kept his windshield clear. And we single parents can't get on with our lives until we learn to get past this preoccupation.

A Biblical Approach

Every time I hear the issue of remarriage discussed, someone says, citing Genesis 2:18, "God is the one who tells us it is not good that man should be alone." And He does. But God doesn't just leave it at that. He has a plan that includes everything we need to consider about the process. Let's take a look at how that plan is revealed in Genesis 2.

- *Verse 7: "And the Lord God formed the man from the dust of the ground and breathed into his nostril the breath of life; and the man became a living being."* God makes each of us totally unique. Psalm 139 says that we are fearfully and wonderfully made. What I look and sound like and how I perceive life are all cut from a design made just for me, and the same is true of you. The first step toward uniting ourselves with another person is to accept the uniqueness God has created. Learn who you are. Examine what He wants from you. Become fulfilled in your individuality.

- *Verse 8: "Now the Lord God had planted a garden in the east, in Eden; and there he put the man he had formed."* God has a place for each of us that has been chosen specifically for us, just as He did for Adam, and we need to give Him free rein to guide us where He wants us to go. That doesn't mean boxing Him in to a limited selection of places we'll accept. It means allowing the creative God of the universe to find a place for you and me that fits our design. When He has complete control in arranging these circumstances, the possibilities are incredible! He can put us in the center of His will, where we'll be happy. The Bible says, "Delight yourself in the Lord and he will give you the desires of your heart" (Psalm 37:4). No contentment is quite like that which comes from being where God wants us to be.

- *Verse 9: "And the Lord God made all kinds of trees grow out of the ground—trees that were pleasing to the eye and good for food. In the middle of the garden were the tree of life and the tree of the knowledge of good and evil."* When God takes charge, He provides for us in every way. We make the choice to abide in Him, and He promises to meet all our "needs according to his glorious riches in Christ Jesus" (Philippians 4:19).

• *Verse 15: "The Lord God took the man and put him in the Garden of Eden to work and take care of it."* God assigns us jobs. No matter how much perfecting He still has to do in each of us, He has something to put us to work on each day. And as long as we're open to His bidding, we can be about our father's business while He takes care of all else.

• *Verse 16: "And the Lord God commanded the man, 'You are free to eat of any tree in the garden.'"* God matures us. He grows us up through our daily reliance on Him. Not only do we learn His provision, but we also learn about obeying His commandments. Selecting the right "fruit" in our daily decisions happens only after seeking His face. He promises that "your ears will hear a voice behind you, saying, 'This is the way; walk in it'" (Isaiah 30:21).

• *Verse 17: "But you must not eat from the tree of the knowledge of good and evil, for when you eat of it you will surely die."* Sin has consequences. "The thief comes only to steal and kill and destroy; I have come that they may have life, and have it to the full" (John 10:10). When we make choices that line up with God's will, we walk with Him. When we sin, we take our hand out of His.

• *Verse 18: "The Lord God said, 'It is not good for the man to be alone. I will make a helper suitable for him.'"* The parts of the plan we've looked at so far constitute a tall order. But if we're doing all those things, then perhaps we're ready to have Him bring someone into our lives—someone who has worked through the same process. Think about the absolute delight of becoming whole in God, then of giving your life to someone who has done the same!

• *Verses 21-22: "So the Lord God caused the man to fall into a deep sleep; and while he was sleeping, he took one of the man's ribs and closed up the place with flesh. Then the Lord God made a woman from the rib he had taken out of the man, and he brought her to the man."* Adam was so busy with his assignments that he didn't notice or interfere with God's matchmaking work. God had found the perfect mate for Adam!

I have a friend who wisely says, "I'd rather want what I don't have than have what I don't want." What a relief to know that God knows what I want—and need—more than I do! I'll let Him take care of that part of my life any day.

Instead of looking for someone to fill the empty place in our lives, let's look to Someone to do it.

❄ ❄ ❄ ❄ ❄ ❄ ❄ ❄

1. What makes you unique?

2. Do you think you're where God wants you to be right now? How do you know?

3. How is God providing for your needs today?

4. What work has God given you to do?

5. What lessons in obedience is God trying to teach you?

"But seek first his kingdom and his righteousness, and all these things will be given to you as well" (Matthew 6:33).

18

A Sweet Fragrance

Do you ever walk through a department store and sample the perfumes on display? When I do, I go home with different fragrances splashed on each wrist and behind both ears. The next morning, I roll over in bed to the smell of all those delightful scents that remain on my pillow and sheets.

God talks about perfumes, too. They didn't have department stores in the days when the Bible was written, but they did have perfumes, and we can learn helpful lessons from what Scripture says about them.

His Scent to Us

We read in Ephesians 5:1-2, "Be imitators of God, therefore, as dearly loved children and live a life of love, just as Christ loved us and gave himself up for us as a fragrant offering and sacrifice to God."

Jesus' sacrificial death to pay the price for our sins was a sweet fragrance to the Father and a love gift to us. As parents, we can understand a little of the pain this meant. God the Father sent Jesus to the earth so He could feel the pains and discomforts, as well as the pleasures, that we experience. He walked the earth for 33 years with no sin in His life. Then He had to die.

The cross. The nails. The agony. God looked down on all this as His one perfect Son was tortured by those He had come to save. How did God receive this injustice? The death of His Son was like an Old

Testament fragrant offering that the priest offered on behalf of the people of Israel—except that this was the ultimate sacrifice, and the last one ever needed.

Our Scent to Him

The Bible also talks about the scent ordinary individuals send up to God when they give sacrificially.

Paul wrote, for example, about help he got from the church at Philippi: "I have received full payment and even more; I am amply supplied, now that I have received from Epaphroditus the gifts you sent. They are a fragrant offering, an acceptable sacrifice, pleasing to God" (Philippians 4:18).

When I was single, living in an apartment and working at my first teaching job, life seemed simple. I had only me to take care of, but I decided I would do something for someone else. I volunteered on Thursday nights at a nursing home up the street. I bought supplies and helped the women make different crafts.

I must admit that after a short time, I did not look forward to that commitment. Tired from a day at work, I wanted to do other, more enjoyable things with my time and money. But every week, no matter how heavy and reluctant the walk to the nursing home, I would float home afterward. Why the difference between going and coming? I knew that somehow my sacrifice was rising to the nostrils of God in a pleasing way.

Our Scent to Others

God's plan for humanity involves using us to reach the world with the gospel of His Son. He tells us that the perfume He is to us and we are to Him is to be shared with everyone. "But thanks be to God, who always leads us in triumphal procession in Christ and through us spreads everywhere the fragrance of the knowledge of him. For we are to God the aroma of Christ among those who are being saved and those who are perishing. To the one we are the smell of death; to the other, the fragrance of life" (2 Corinthians 2:14-16).

In a "stinky" world with foul things happening all around us, God offers a sweet smell to all through His people. As His representatives, we always carry an odor to those we meet.

One day my children and I were able to share God's sweet odor with a man on the highway. He entered the interstate suddenly, his car out of control. As his vehicle headed perpendicular to the flow of the traffic and toward a cement wall, the children and I shot up desperate prayers. Miraculously, the car turned just before it hit the wall (or any other cars), and the man eventually pulled it back under control.

We took the same exit as that driver, and as we both pulled up to the red light at the end of the ramp, I rolled down my window and motioned for the man to do the same.

"We were praying for you back there—I mean really praying," I told him.

Still visibly shaken, he thanked me.

That man might never again see the family that pulled away in the dirty, little, white car, but he will always smell the fragrance that we left from the hand of God in our lives.

Our Failures

Sometimes, however, the odor we emit is not pleasant. Sometimes we downright stink.

I remember a time just three months after my divorce was final. The day was Thursday, and we had just buried my dad. I dropped the children off at their father's for the weekend and made my way back home.

I walked into our empty apartment. I had things to do but no motivation to get started. I thought, *What do I have left? Who cares for me, anyway?*

As I was lost in the depths of self-pity, my telephone rang. The caller was a man I had done some business with, but this call was strictly pleasure. We talked for a few minutes, and then he told me he was married—and I didn't hang up. I stayed on the phone with this welcome human voice for a few more minutes.

The next day, he showed up at my door. I didn't know what to do. I had never faced a temptation like this before. I knew well what it felt like to be on the victim's end of adultery, but now I was in the pit of despair.

I did two things right during that time of temptation, however. First, I talked openly to a couple of friends who held me accountable for my actions and gave me sound direction. Second, I talked to God often. I told Him what I was facing and what a crummy job I was doing in handling this problem.

"But if You are the Lord of my life," I prayed, "please be strong for me now."

That's when I read about perfume one more time: "As dead flies give perfume a bad smell, so a little folly outweighs wisdom and honor" (Ecclesiastes 10:1).

God didn't smack me around and tell me what a dummy I was. He was saying, "Lynda, all the good things you stand for will be destroyed if you let this one temptation become sin in your life."

With that loving admonition and continued guidance from my accountability friends, I stopped the situation without sin ever occurring.

Our Prayers

Just as I have a favorite perfume at the department store, so I have a favorite passage about perfume in the Bible; it relates to our prayers. Just look at this:

"Another angel, who had a golden censer, came and stood at the altar. He was given much incense to offer, with the prayers of all the saints, on the golden altar before the throne. The smoke of the incense, together with the prayers of the saints, went up before God from the angel's hand" (Revelation 8:3-4).

One day my son, Clint, came home from school crying. A boy in his class was making fun of him. I showed him Revelation 8:3-4, assuring him, "God hears our prayers as soon as we say them, and they are pleasing to Him." Then Clint and I prayed.

The next day, he came home wearing a smile and told me how the boy had been nicer to him and even shared part of his lunch. Soon my daughter Courtney walked into the kitchen and complained about a conflict she was also having at school. Clint reached up and put his right arm around his sister's shoulder. "Tell you what you gotta do . . ." he began as they walked away together.

Not all our prayers are answered that quickly or simply, and some appear as though they're not being answered at all. But as Clint learned that day, God hears every time we pray. The angels personally deliver the words from our mouth to the nostrils of God.

Sometimes we represent God well to the world, and sometimes we stink at it. But always, our prayers are a fragrance to Him. That makes me want to "Be [an] imitator of God . . . and live a life of love, just as Christ loved us and gave himself up for us as a fragrant offering and sacrifice to God." What about you?

❈　❈　❈　❈　❈　❈　❈　❈

1. How are you a fragrance of God in your home? at work? in your neighborhood? at church?

2. How can you "smell" better?

"But thanks be to God, who always leads us in triumphal procession in Christ and through us spreads everywhere the fragrance of the knowledge of him" (2 Corinthians 2:14).

19

Historical Markers
Ahead

On a summer trip to South Dakota a few years ago, my children and I visited Mount Rushmore. As we approached that spectacular landmark, we saw a sign that said, "Historical Marker Ahead."

I pulled the van to a stop. On a bronze plaque, we read that Gutzon and Lincoln Borglum carved the faces of four presidents into the granite of the Black Hills mountain over a 14-year period. The site became more than a tourist stop after we read that marker—it became a timeless memorial for us.

Other memorials have affected my life through the years. Several of them are found in the Bible. Markers were created by individuals to commemorate events or accomplishments they didn't want successive generations to forget.

Moses was one of the first who left behind such a memorial. Perhaps you're familiar with the story of the Exodus. Because the Egyptians refused to comply with God's command to free the people of Israel, God sent several plagues. Just before the last plague came upon the land, Moses directed that blood be put on the doorposts of the Israelite homes so that the angel of death "passed over" them. God said, "Obey these instructions as a lasting ordinance for you and your descendants. When you enter the land that the Lord will give you as he promised, observe this ceremony. And when your children ask you, 'What does this ceremony mean to you?' then tell them, 'It is the Passover sacrifice'" (Exodus 12:24-27).

Another memorial maker was Joshua. He led the Israelites into the Promised Land when God rolled back the Jordan River so the Israelites could cross on dry ground. Once on the other side, Joshua instructed the tribes of Israel to take stones from the river and place them for a memorial. "to serve as a sign among you. In the future, when your children ask you, 'What do these stones mean?' tell them that the flow of the Jordan was cut off before the ark of the covenant of the Lord" (Joshua 4:6-7).

The prophet Samuel also set up a memorial. The men of Israel went out of the town of Mizpah and defeated the Philistines. "Then Samuel took a stone and set it up between Mizpah and Shen. He named it Ebenezer, saying, 'Thus far has the Lord helped us'" (1 Samuel 7:12).

Growing Up with Memorials

My mom and dad became Christians when I was six months old. From that point on, they sought to learn everything they could about God and to raise my older sister and me and six younger siblings to know the Lord.

Despite my parents' newfound reliance on Christ, things were never easy. We battled financial hardships, health problems, and other difficulties. Yet today, I can look over the lives of each of my brothers and sisters, as well as my own, and see memorials that show how God has remained faithful.

One cold winter day in our small Ohio town, for example, I stepped off the afternoon school bus onto the snow-covered ground. As I strolled toward my home, my eyes traveled to one of the honey locust trees in our front yard. A clump of locust blossoms hung amid the barren branches. Hardly believing what I saw, I found my dad's clippers and ladder, climbed up to the branches, and cut off the unusual prize. I wrote about it in my English class the next day.

Twenty years later, when I found myself in the middle of a divorce, I took the dreaded drive to the attorney's office to do what I had been forced to do. Springtime had arrived, and signs of new life were everywhere along the way. My heart, however, only knew heaviness.

I rolled down the window for a breath of fresh air. Suddenly, I smelled an aroma from deep in my past. There beside the road was a grove of honey locust trees, covered with clumps of blossoms. That wonderful aroma filled the car and lifted my tired heart as it seemed to say to me, *There is a clump of locust blossoms amid all this barrenness today.*

Seeing those locust blossoms became my reminder, my memorial.

Today's Memorials

My parents blazed a trail for me in their walk with God. One day at a time, they learned to call on the Lord and rely on Him in all circumstances. They weren't fortunate enough to have had Christian parents themselves, but I was. Knowing I could ask for God's help in everything—from a spelling test in school to the major decisions that would shape my future—became a way of life for me.

As a second-generation Christian now raising a third, my challenge is the same as it was for my parents. When God teaches me He is a God who provides by making our finances stretch, I relate this fact to the kids. When He shows me His power to heal by touching the fevered brow of one of my children, they discover it, too. When they see me go to Him for wisdom and guidance and then watch Him come through, my children learn to do the same in their own lives. And when my children ask me "What does this memorial mean?" I don't hesitate to tell them.

A Lasting Ordinance

As much as I've seen the miracles and power of God, I still get stumped when new problems arise.

Not long ago, I called my mom with a concern about my family. I explained how I had prayed and felt that God had not answered. Mom said with confidence, "Lynda, I already prayed about that the other night before going to sleep. I remember the spot on the wall I looked at as I gave all to Him. Now every time I look at that spot, I remember that my concern is already His!"

Yesterday's problems are not all solved for me, and today brings new issues of its own. But I move confidently ahead, knowing that others have walked before me—Moses, Joshua, Samuel, and Mom and Dad among them. They learned that He is faithful. And they've left me memorials that say: "This is what happened. This is what He did here. Build on it, use it, and never, never forget it."

Thus, when I see the stones or smell the clump of locust blossoms, it becomes easier to remember my own spots on the wall where I gave all my concerns to Him. They're His. I'm His. And that's all that matters.

✄ ✄ ✄ ✄ ✄ ✄ ✄ ✄

As you face the daily issues of single parenting, I encourage you to remember the memorials—both those in Scripture and those you can find in your own experience.

1. Take some time to remember past victories in your life. Recall, too, the dates those victories took place.

2. Now, take some time and list the battles you are facing today. What is happening that only God can fix?

3. Identify a new memorial—your own Ebenezer—in the lives of you and your children. Find your spot on the wall—something that you can look at to remind you, "Thus far has the Lord helped us." Then move forward with confidence, remembering that those issues belong to Him.

"Watch yourselves closely so that you do not forget the things your eyes have seen or let them slip from your heart as long as you live. Teach them to your children and to their children after them" (Deuteronomy 4:9).

20

A Giant and Still
Growing

When I was a teenager, I baby-sat for a family at their grandparents' summer cottage in Michigan. They took great delight in notching the pine kitchen door frame with measurements of the grandchildren's growth each season. Some of the year-to-year changes were amazing, while others were barely discernible.

I have sometimes wondered how we would measure up if God used a door frame to determine our yearly spiritual growth. We mature as we learn more about Him through His Word and through trusting in His faithfulness. Have we advanced in this area, or is our growth hardly measurable as we wrestle with the same hang-ups we had five years ago?

I've known people whose growth in the Lord was obvious and constant. My dad was one of them. He left his mark on all who knew him, especially on his family. And his example challenged me to leave to my children a life marked by growth and consistency. I wrote this tribute to my dad as seen through my brother Philip's eyes.

> The late afternoon rays of the autumn sun lay warm upon my hair as I played with my truck in the sand. Suddenly, I heard footsteps rustling through the leaves. A long shadow appeared as my dad reached out with both arms and scooped me up, up, up into the air and crushed me with a hug.

Dad began to sing "Jesus Loves Me, This I Know" as we set out for our daily walk to visit the black-and-white cows across the road. His walk was not swift, but I loved the gentle sway of his giant stride that brought us there quickly. The cows stared with their customary curiosity as they continued to chew their cud. Dad told me how the cows searched carefully for good grazing but quickly returned to the barn when the master called.

One day when I was seven, my dad played ball with me in the yard. The trees were our bases. No matter where I made my pitch, Dad extended his great arms and made contact with his bat. When I retrieved the ball, he slowed down and pretended to be surprised as I tagged him out and we fell laughing into the grass.

Dad taught my teenage Sunday school class. He stood tall as he shared his great knowledge and showed us the way to the cross and a life with Jesus. I sometimes talked and fooled around with my friends and failed to listen to what Dad told us. But I saw a consistency in what he said and what I saw him do as he studied his Bible each night and knelt beside his bed in prayer.

Others also saw the giant in my dad. They called him often for prayer and counsel. Many times I heard him return after ministering to someone through the night just in time to go to his job.

I traveled one day as a man to be with my dad at his bedside. It was hard for me to see this giant sick and unable to do all the things I remembered. *What was Dad's secret,* I wondered, *to being so big? Why didn't he topple as so many other great men have? How has he managed to remain a spiritual giant?*

I walked toward his room but stopped at his door as I heard him pray.

". . . and Lord, for Mary. She needs a touch in her body as she undergoes this surgery. Be with my children, each and every one of them, as they face decisions they must make. And God, make me a faithful servant. Draw me closer to be more like You."

I walked into the room. His eyes filled with tears, and a weak smile touched his lips. Giant arms reached out feebly to embrace me. We talked. We cried. Then Dad slept.

As he did, I reached over to his side and picked up his Bible. It was open to a page that was clearly marked. "But I keep under my body and bring it into subjection: lest that by any means, when I have preached to others, I myself should be a castaway" (1 Corinthians 9:27, KJV).

I looked at my dad's labored breathing, and suddenly I knew his secret. He was a giant who was still growing. He daily measured himself by standing next to God, where anyone appears small. He continued to search out better pasture and responded dutifully to the master, like the cows he once described. He opened himself so God could make him better at all he did. And he devoted himself to Bible reading and prayer, the most fertile grounds in which to grow.

Dad never woke from his sleep that afternoon but passed on to be with his Lord. As I walked from his room into the cool spring air, I realized God had been building the inner part of my dad even up to the hour he died. That was what made him a giant.

I wiped the tears from my eyes as I heard someone calling,

"Daddy! Daddy!" My gaze fell upon a small boy running across the lawn with his arms outstretched. The wind tousled my son's hair, and the sun seemed to follow him with its rays. When he reached me, he put his head back as far as he could and looked up at me with smiling eyes. He jumped into my arms, and I scooped him up, up, up into the air. I crushed him with a big hug. "Some day," he said, "I want to be a giant just like you, Daddy."

We walked away together, and I heard myself humming, "Jesus Loves Me, This I Know."

No one sees or hears our Christian witness more clearly than do our children. Based on your children's observations of you, do they see the Christian life as:

• involving compromise, or is it consistent and Christlike in all situations?

• being stagnant, no further along than it was last year, or is it vibrant and dynamic, with the growth clearly visible?

• boring, unexciting, and irrelevant, or is it constantly new, exhilarating, and applicable to everyday concerns?

What behaviors in you cause them to believe as they do?
A song comes to mind:

May all who come behind us find us faithful.
May the fire of our devotion light their way.
May the footprints that we leave,
Lead them to believe.

And the lives we live inspire them to obey.

Oh, may all who come behind us find us faithful.

*(Words and music by Jon Mohr. Copyright © 1987 Jonathan Mark Music
ASCAP and Birdwing Music ASCAP. All rights reserved. Used by permission.)*

As moms and dads, you and I seek to be the best cooks, listeners, and self-esteem builders we can be. But what spiritual footprints are we leaving for our children? Will those who are coming behind us find us faithful?

What can you do to revive or enhance your spiritual witness to your children? Name specific ways by which you can become a spiritual giant to them.

"Be faithful, even to the point of death, and I will give you the crown of life" (Revelation 2:10).

21

God's Army

In fifth grade, I was the teacher's pet. I'll never forget nine months of getting to write the assignments on the board, running errands, and doing special favors throughout the day. The other kids never seemed to notice. They probably got their chance another year with another teacher. But fifth grade was mine, all mine.

I used to wonder what brought me such favor. Was it that she knew my parents? Was it my charming adolescent personality or my gangly appearance? What did I do to deserve such attention from her?

As an adult, I've also wondered what causes God to use certain people. Is it their background? Their personalities or appearance? As I studied the story of Gideon in the book of Judges (chapters 6–7), I began to get some answers. Gideon presented thousands of men before the Lord to serve in His army, but God chose only 300. What criteria did He use?

The Fearful

Gideon counted 32,000 men in his Israelite army ready to fight the Midianites. But God told him the number needed to be reduced so Israel would not attribute its coming victory to a large army. To do this, God told Gideon to ask anyone who was afraid to go home.

Gideon obeyed. I'm sure he probably thought, *This is good. We'll get rid of a few hundred cowards.* But he probably questioned whether he had heard correctly from the Lord when 22,000 fearful men turned back.

How would he ever fight the enemy with only 10,000 men, regardless of how fearless they were? But Gideon forged ahead, willing to attempt it with the Lord on his side. They set their faces toward the battle lines. Then God lowered another boom.

The Distracted

God next told Gideon, "There are still too many men. Take them down to the water, and I will sift them for you there. If I say, 'This one shall go with you,' he shall go; but if I say, 'This one shall not go with you,' he shall not go" (Judges 7:4).

Gideon did as he was asked. He took the men to the water. There God spoke to him again: "Separate those who lap the water with their tongues like a dog from those who kneel down to drink" (Judges 7:5). Only 300 men cupped water with their hands and brought them to their mouths. The rest got down on their knees to drink.

I know a man who served in the 101st Squadron in Vietnam. He relates that when his platoon was advancing toward the enemy, and they arrived at a stream to drink, they had to do so without bending over so as not to lose their stride.

This meant bringing the water up to their mouths. If a man stooped down and lapped the water, he was dropping his guard and endangering the whole platoon. Therefore, the best soldiers were those who kept their heads up and their eyes open and did not neglect their mission to satisfy their own needs.

"The Lord said to Gideon, 'With the three hundred men that lapped I will save you and give the Midianites into your hands. Let all the other men go, each to his own place'" (Judges 7:7).

The Remnant Then and Now

Gideon's army was now cut from 32,000 to 300 men. The first 22,000 had their eyes and hearts frozen in fear of the enemy. These men were so focused on their own limited abilities that they failed to see the omnipotence of God. The remaining 9,700 had their attention on themselves and their needs rather than on the mission their army had set out to accomplish. God had told Gideon He would test them all. Only 300 men passed and moved forward.

I can't help but wonder if I would have been eliminated that day. I am often afraid, and I occupy myself with so many things. The Bible tells us that whatever is important to us is where we will spend our time and efforts (see Matthew 6:21). Would my self-preoccupation have caused me to stop at the river and drink with little thought for the work I was called to do?

In our own day, we seldom remember that we are temporary residents here on earth, just passing through on our way to heaven, our eternal home. To give attention to the things of God is a daily battle. Our own lives and needs—even our God-given relationships—can become hindrances to our praise, worship, and service to God when we don't center our attention on Him.

I've learned that my time with God is the most integral part of my day. It makes me a better mom. I listen more, feel greater contentment, have deeper insights, and commit to fewer of my own agendas. Even the other areas of my life, like my job or housecleaning, have a way of getting done as I consistently put the Lord in charge of each day.

God's army comprises those few who have their eyes, hearts, and efforts focused on God.

The Victory

"Dividing the three hundred men into three companies, he placed trumpets and empty jars in the hands of all of them, with torches inside. 'Watch me,' he told them. 'Follow my lead. When I get to the edge of the camp, do exactly as I do. When I and all who are with me blow our trumpets, then from all around the camp blow yours and shout, "For the Lord and for Gideon"'" (Judges 7:16-17).

Gideon and his men reached the edge of the camp and began their watch. "The three companies blew the trumpets and smashed the jars" (Judges 7:20). They grasped the torches in their left hands and blew the trumpets with their right hands, saying, "A sword for the Lord and for Gideon." The Midianites ran, crying as they fled. They even turned on each other with their swords.

Where would you and I have ended up if we were among the original 32,000 men of Israel? Would we have trembled in fear of evil rather than trust in the power of God? Would we have been so caught up in our own needs that we couldn't stay focused on God? At the stream, would we have served ourselves only or lifted the water to our mouths and marched on to fulfill the mission? Would we have cast our torches into the night?

God could have accomplished the same end with all 32,000 of Gideon's men. But by their choice, most missed the excitement of victory. Every day and everywhere, there are people who will live forever because someone remained faithful in God's army. Can you and I forget our fears, pull out our torches, share our faith, and put our lives on the line?

❈ ❈ ❈ ❈ ❈ ❈ ❈ ❈

1. Describe the battlefield to which God has called you.

2. What fears do you feel?

3. The Bible says to cast all your fears on Him because He cares for you (see 1 Peter 5:7). Do that today.

4. What consumes your time and distracts you from the battle at hand? Matthew 6 tells us not to be worried about our lives. God will take care of everything. List the things that preoccupy you in this area.

5. Now give everything to God and march on to victory.

"For many are invited, but few are chosen" (Matthew 22:14).

22

Making Your Own
Wilderness Journey

"If you lived through the Depression as I did, you wouldn't waste this food," my mother often said to us kids while we were growing up. She would continue with specific stories, but my seven brothers and sisters and I tuned her out as we went about our merry, carefree ways. Her vivid accounts weren't real to us because we hadn't experienced them firsthand. We knew about the events only through what we heard. It wasn't until we had gone through our own difficulties that many of our mother's words came back to us with real meaning.

I found a personal relationship with God when I became a single mom of three babies. In the early days of looking to Him for guidance, my allegiance wasn't strong. I trusted little, prayed with uncertainty, and wondered if my problems were of concern to Him.

My mom and dad had served Him with fervor since I was six months old. In raising me, they taught me about God, took me to church, and exposed me to others who believed. At times they voiced concern about my conduct, what I was listening to, who I was hanging around with, or how little time I was spending with God. I had not yet forged my own relationship with Him.

Once during Bible study in our living room, tears filled my mother's eyes as she taught us a passage from Song of Songs 3:1-4. She asked us to memorize those words that summed up the intense love relationship she had found with Jesus Christ. I learned by heart words that held little meaning. Like my ignorance of the Great Depression, I had no firsthand experience of the things that made Solomon's words real.

The years following my surrender to Christ have been hard in countless ways, but I have found God faithful. Through it all, I've learned to trust thoroughly, pray with certainty, and, as instructed in 1 Peter 5:7, give all my worries to Him.

Today I find myself in the place Mom and Dad were many years ago. I'm imparting all I can to my children while they're still under my roof. I, too, complain about their conduct, what they listen to, who they hang around with, and how little time they spend with God. Sometimes I grow fearful of what could happen to them. But recently I've been learning what God says about these rites of passage. Knowing His wisdom has helped me release unrealistic expectations for myself *and* for my kids.

Why the Tough Times?

When we're young and our futures lie before us, we often don't think about hard times. The day I married, I thought I would never need God in any significant way. Things were going well, and I was making my own choices. But then the tough times came. Difficulties arose that were beyond my control. I needed help.

Why couldn't I have learned about tough times through others' experiences? Why not just read about crummy places and assimilate the lessons? The answer is found in Deuteronomy 8:2: "Remember how the Lord your God led you all the way in the desert these forty years, to humble you and to test you in order to know what was in your heart, whether or not you would keep his commands."

God puts us through our own wilderness experiences to humble us and cause us to see that we can't go it alone. That way, we learn to rely on Him. He also uses tough times to test us. As C. S. Lewis said, "God whispers to us in our pleasures . . . but shouts in our pain. It is His megaphone to rouse a deaf world." If we let it, pain brings about strength, courage, and character. These traits can never be acquired vicariously. Tough experiences create the opportunity to make a deliberate decision for Christ. He wants us to choose Him freely out of our need.

What Should Parents Do?

So how do we parents help our children who haven't yet gone through their own wilderness experiences? We find some answers in Deuteronomy 11.

> Love the Lord your God and keep his requirements, his decrees, his laws and his commands always. Remember today that your children were not the ones who saw and experienced the discipline of the Lord your God: his majesty, his mighty hand, his outstretched arm; the signs he performed and the things he did in the heart of Egypt. . . . It was not your children who saw what he did for you in the desert until you arrived at this place. . . . But it was your own eyes that saw all these great things the Lord has done. (verses 1-3,5,7)

As that passage indicates, God wants us first to live godly lives. We are to know His laws and model obedience to them as examples to our children. But then He wants us to understand that our kids won't automatically inherit our enthusiasm for God. I didn't learn frugality through my mom's stories of the Great Depression but through my own lean times. Likewise, my kids won't automatically offer undying devotion to Him because of what I've gone through. We Hunter kids encountered difficulties of our own that honed our beliefs, and my children will experience their own wildernesses where they will learn a true trust in God.

Scripture goes on to tell us to share what we know with our children every day in every way, then wait for God to do the rest:

> Fix these words of mine in your hearts and minds; tie them as symbols on your hands and bind them on your foreheads. Teach them to your children, talking about them when you sit at home and when you walk along the road, when you lie down and when you get up. Write them on the doorframes of your houses and on your gates, so that your days and the days of your children may be many in the land that the Lord swore to give your forefathers, as many as the days that the heavens are above the earth. (Deuteronomy 11:18-21)

God is at work in our children to help them remember the source of their early instruction. He's able to bring recall and application to what our kids have learned. He reminds them that our homes were built brick by brick through trusting in God, and He lets them know our health and well-being come only from Him. They will learn that they can't go it alone any more than could the generations before them.

Been There and Back

During a recent Bible study with my children, I sat in front of them and opened my mouth to speak. Suddenly I was the little girl listening to my own mother's words from the Song of Songs: "All night long on my bed I looked for the one my heart loves; I looked for him but did not find him."

I stopped to wipe the tears that clouded my eyes.

"I will get up now and go about the city, through its streets and squares; I will search for the one my heart loves.

"So I looked for him but did not find him. The watchmen found me as they made their rounds in the city. 'Have you seen the one my heart loves?'"

Memories of my own wilderness experiences came flooding back.

"Scarcely had I passed them when I found the one my heart loves. I held him and would not let him go till I had brought him into my mother's house, and to the room of the one who conceived me" (Song of Songs 3:1-4).

I finished the words that once belonged to my mother and now belonged to me. This time they were real and came from a heart that was reserved only for God. I am confident that one day the words will belong to my children—after they have experienced their own wildernesses and have found their own love relationship with Him. In the meantime, I'll just keep talking about His words while my children sit at home and when they walk along the road, when they lie down and when they get up, so that my days and the days of my children may b many in the land.

✄ ✄ ✄ ✄ ✄ ✄ ✄ ✄

Reflect on your own wilderness experiences, and answer these questions:

1. In what ways has God humbled and tested you? What did He find in your heart?

2. Have you loved the Lord and kept His commands as examples to your children? Are there ways you can do this better?

3. In what ways did you teach God's principles to your kids when they were young? How can you adapt these methods now that they're older?

4. Pray this prayer with confidence:

"God, I know You are at work in my children's lives. Talk to them, instruct them, and bring to mind what they should know. Meanwhile, help me to teach and model Your principles while I rest in the knowledge that You are in control. I thank You because You are bigger than all our circumstances, and because You want my children to be with You even more than I want it. I love You for that. Amen."

"When your son asks you, 'What is the meaning of the stipulations, decrees and laws the Lord our God has commanded you?' tell him . . ." (Deuteronomy 6:20-21).

23

Making a House
a Home

One summer afternoon, my children and I were invited to the home of someone I had met at the university where I taught. I felt envious of the original Picasso painting and the extravagant furnishings in this posh townhouse in a prestigious neighborhood.

Back at home later that evening, my family prepared for bed. My older daughter, Ashley, came into my room to say good night. As she turned to leave, she said, "Mom, Mrs. Gilbert has a beautiful *house,* but we have a beautiful *home.*"

Ashley's words were a compliment to me for having raised my children alone for six years. Although I knew everything in our home was not perfect, something we shared as a family made her see a difference.

But creating a nurturing home has not come easily for me. Since becoming a single parent, I've sought direction from the Bible. I've been delighted by the practical and humorous ways God has taught me what I need to know. I found one passage in Job that showed me even some animals struggle with making a "house" a "home."

The Ostrich

"She lays her eggs on the ground and lets them warm in the sand, unmindful that a foot may crush them, that some wild animal may trample them. She treats her young harshly, as if they were not hers; she doesn't care that her labor was in vain, for God did not endow her with wisdom or give her a share of good sense" (Job 39:14-17).

The ostrich is polygamous and not the kind of species to make strong commitments. The female ostrich moves from one mate to another, and the male fertilizes clutches of eggs with several different females. Each female lays about 15 eggs in shallow depressions in dry, sandy African soil, where they're vulnerable to being stepped on or eaten. Yet once they're laid, the mother often abandons them and goes about her merry way.

For these reasons, few of the eggs survive. The motherless babies that are born have no one to nurture them or teach them what they need to know. They learn quickly to fend for themselves and eat anything they can find.

Clearly, the ostrich's home is not one to emulate.

The Eagle

"Does the eagle soar at your command and build his nest on high? He dwells on a cliff and stays there at night; a rocky crag is his stronghold. From there he seeks out his food; his eyes detect it from afar. His young ones feast on blood, and where the slain are, there is he" (Job 39:27-30).

Unlike the ostrich, the eagle is monogamous. Eagles not only mate for life, but they usually occupy the same nest year after year, too. Their nests are in high trees or on remote cliffs and consist of large sticks padded with leaves and grass for comfort. The female continues to make home improvements each year—one nest discovered in Ohio was 36 years old and weighed almost a ton.

The mountains where eagles' nests are found are far from the bustling world into which ostriches are born. The eaglets are greeted with a breeze that whistles through the trees, interrupted only occasionally by other sounds of nature.

The parent eagles feed the downy young for up to 130 days before sending them out on their own. During that time in their quiet, orderly homes, the eaglets are taught survival skills by Mom and Dad. They can see with their keen eyes for up to 16 miles.

From their home on high, the eaglet is taught to spot its prey, dive at its surprised victims, grab the food in its strong talons, and bring it back home to devour. The eaglet is also taught to see where dangers lie. Finally, from the security of its home, the eaglet has a clear perspective on what lies above. The heavens, the sky, the big picture are part of everything eaglets see from the day they are born.

My Place

I often lie on my bed at night, assessing my performance as a mom that day. Sometimes I can be proud of the verdict. Other times, like the ostrich, I want to stick my head in the sand. I find myself thinking about the ostrich and the eagle and asking myself these questions:

• Where have I chosen to build our home? Is it a safe environment like the eagle's nest, conducive to healthy physical and Christian growth?

• Am I committed to my children and their development? Or, like the ostrich, am I content to let them go off and do their own things?

• Am I feeding them food—natural and spiritual—that builds strong and godly men and women? Or am I leaving them to feed on whatever they can find?

• Do I, like the eagle, make daily improvements in our home for comfort and to fit our growing needs?

• Am I creative and energetic in equipping them with skills to seek out the good and avoid the bad?

"By Wisdom a House Is Built"

The difference between the eagle and the ostrich is wisdom.

Knowledge is knowing what's best; understanding is making sense out of what we know. But wisdom puts the thoughts into action. As parents, we may know the best ways to raise our kids and even understand why those ways are best. But we need wisdom to make it all work.

One afternoon, my son, Clint, came home from kindergarten. I took him to the backyard to play while I carried my briefcase filled with paperwork.

I had just settled down at the picnic table to begin the first task when Clint came running across the yard, his arms laden with small tree branches. "Mommy," he said, "show me how to make something with my sticks."

I took another look at several memos and then at his big, brown eyes, wide with anticipation.

I walked into the house and gathered glue and a pair of scissors. Clint and I then spent the afternoon constructing a house and lots of special memories.

That night, he came to kiss me good night. He added a warm hug and said, "That's for helping me make something with my sticks today."

I had the *knowledge* that it was best to spend time with my son. I even *understood* the reasons. But thanks to the *wisdom* that God gave me, I was able to do it as well.

I didn't finish my paperwork that day. As a matter of fact, I don't even know what happened to the list. But I nurtured and guided and loved my son so that when he's a dad, he will also know how to nurture and guide and love.

Those are the things that make our house a home. That's what wisdom does.

✖ ✖ ✖ ✖ ✖ ✖ ✖ ✖

In James 1:5 we read, "If any of you lacks wisdom, he should ask God, who gives generously to all without finding fault, and it will be given to him."

Be bold. Be specific. Tell God three ways you need wisdom today for making your house a home. (You can write them out below). Then thank Him for giving generously to that need.

1.

2.

3.

"By wisdom a house is built" (Proverbs 24:3).

24

Visitors of Hope

Timothy wept. He fingered the bottle of sleeping pills that sat on the nightstand. Silent walls in his silent apartment brought memories of his children, now gone. His once-busy schedule was now empty. How different things were.

He had been sure he was justified, though he knew it wasn't right. The woman he had become involved with had appreciated him. She had recognized that his talents weren't limited to breadwinning. She had made him feel good about himself. But not now. She was gone, and so were his wife, his marriage, and his children.

Timothy clutched the pills close to his chest. *I have no reason to live,* he thought. *Wouldn't my children be better off with a dead father than with a stupid, absent one?*

"Can You ever forgive me, God?" Timothy said aloud as he buried his head in the pillow and spilled more tears. Finally he succumbed to exhaustion.

Meet Grace

Sleep was interrupted. "Timothy," he heard.

He opened his eyes to two women standing in his room. The closest one spoke first: "I've come with a message from God. 'My grace is sufficient for you, for my power is made perfect in weakness'" (2 Corinthians 12:9).

"Who are you?" Timothy asked.

"I am Grace," was the simple reply. "I've been sent today loaded down with love. Today you are forgiven, my son. And tomorrow and all the days to come, I'll still be with you to help you live your life for God."

"But, but . . ." stammered Timothy. "I've done awful things. I've lied. I've betrayed. I've committed adultery. Everything I had is lost."

"You're not the first, nor will you be the last," said Grace. "Remember Hebrews 11 that talks about the great heroes of the faith? Do you think all those people were perfect?

"Abraham's lie to the king of Egypt saying that his wife was his sister is not recorded in Hebrews 11, though Abraham is. The time his faith was weak and he took Hagar as a wife because he didn't believe God's promise that Sarah would bear him a child wasn't recorded there either. God says, 'Their sins and lawless acts I will remember no more' (Hebrews 10:17). God does not record failure in heaven once that failure is forgiven!

"And we mustn't forget Rahab," Grace continued. "'By faith the prostitute Rahab, because she welcomed the spies, was not killed with those who were disobedient' (Hebrews 11:31). It was from her lineage that Jesus, the Son of God, eventually came. All from a prostitute—a forgiven prostitute!"

"But even if God forgives me and I forgive myself, what about my family?" Timothy asked. "How will my children ever forgive me?"

"That's were Mercy comes in."

Enter Mercy

"Meet Mercy," said Grace.

Mercy held out her arms.

"I've come," said Mercy, "to bring compassion to all who are forgiven but who are still needy, distressed, or suffering. God wants to draw close to you in spite of your mistakes. I'm here to bring big things from God, though you deserve little. In the midst of your faithlessness, His faithfulness continues."

Timothy was overwhelmed. "But I don't deserve this!" he protested.

"If you deserved it," she answered, "you wouldn't need mercy. That's the nature of who I am."

"Do you mean my wife and children will return?" Timothy asked.

"That I don't know. But God will certainly walk with you in whatever lies ahead. He will help you and bless you with all that concerns you—and that includes your children. God will give you what it takes, but you must rise up, be strong, and be the daddy you've been called to be."

Grace and Mercy backed away.

"Don't go!" Timothy pleaded. "How will I keep going once you're gone? What will sustain me? How will I know what to do?"

Grace answered, "I came to convey God's forgiveness for your sins. Mercy brings goodness in your distress. But God leaves this message and His Word to help you go on: 'Peace I leave with you; my peace I give you. I do not give to you as the world gives. Do not let your [heart] be troubled and do not be afraid' (John 14:27). Grace and mercy are acts of God, and His peace enters the heart of man as a result. God leaves His peace with you always, Timothy."

With those words, Grace and Mercy were gone.

Peace at Last

Timothy opened his eyes. *Where am I?* he wondered. He saw the sleeping pills lying on the floor. His incredible night experience came flooding back. Then fear rose inside him. *What if this was just a dream? Can I really do it alone?*

With those questions, he remembered Grace's parting words: "But God leaves this message and His Word to help you go on."

Timothy reached over and picked up his Bible. It opened to 2 Timothy 1:2, and he read: "To Timothy, my dear son: Grace, mercy and peace from God the Father and Christ Jesus our Lord."

Thanks to Grace and Mercy, Timothy was able to go on.

❧ ❧ ❧ ❧ ❧ ❧ ❧ ❧

Proverbs 31 was written by King Lemuel to his mother. It describes her as worth far more than rubies; as bringing good, not harm; as providing food for her family. And who was Lemuel? Most Bible scholars believe he was Solomon, whose mother was Bathsheba—the same one who had an adulterous affair with David. Yet Grace and Mercy also paid visits to Bathsheba and David, and their sins became something of the past.

Have you made some mistake in the past that continues to haunt you? If so, do the following:

1. Ask for God's grace. It's time to let go. Begin by confessing your sins to Him. Be specific. Describe the things you need forgiveness for.

2. Ask for God's mercy. It will help you through the battles to come.

3. Ask for God's peace. Don't let Satan beat you over the head anymore with your mistakes.

"As far as the east is from the west, so far has he removed our transgressions from us" (Psalm 103:12).

25

When the Bottom
Drops Out

When I was a child, one of the favorite desserts my mother would make for my seven siblings and me was warm blackberry dumplings over ice cream. The trouble with blackberries, however, is that they come from the prickliest, weediest, most chigger-infested part of the woods.

One summer day, over my protestation that I suddenly didn't like blackberry dumplings, Mother loaded me and the pails and buckets into the back of our old Ford station wagon. Then she sent Dad and me off to pick more berries.

We got an early start, but the sun was soon burning down on my head, my dark hair intensifying the heat. I stooped, tugged, bent, and stretched to reach the most choice produce I could find. After two hours of this, I decided to take a break. Standing on top of a small knoll, I put the last handful of blackberries into the bucket that was fastened with a belt around my waist.

All at once, without warning, the bucket bottom gave way, and out fell my two hours of labor. The berries seemed to roll one by one in slow motion to the foot of the hill. Instead of enjoying the break I had planned, I spent time running, slipping, and sliding down the bank, trying to salvage the fruit I had spilled. . . .

I grew up and went to college. I was able to work and put myself through, thanks to living at home. In three years, I became the first college graduate in the history of either my dad's or my mom's families. After a December graduation, I landed my first teaching job. Five years later, I said yes to a man whom I was dating and prepared to fill my bucket of life even fuller.

We married in a beautiful November wedding. Two years later, our first daughter, Ashley, was born; and two years after that, another daughter, Courtney, graced our lives. By the time our third child was on his way, the bottom dropped out of my entire life. My husband left. Like the blackberries I watched roll down the hill, everything I had worked so hard to build landed in a heap at my feet.

When All Was Lost

The disciples of Jesus also knew what it meant, after a three-year adventure, to have the bottom drop out.

Jesus had called Simon Peter and his brother Andrew from the fishing boat they worked on, Matthew from the taxes he collected, James and John from mending their nets, and seven other men from the places where they were busy with their lives. They had each turned in their resignations, the security of the company car and health insurance, to follow a man they didn't really understand toward a destination of which they were not certain.

But they did it. Good and bad days followed. Sometimes they were sure they had made the right choice, and other times they would have given anything for a home-cooked meal and a real paycheck.

Jesus kept them going, however. Every time they felt like giving up and going home, He broke the monotony of the day by doing something like raising the dead or changing water into wine. They were okay as long as Jesus was sticking around and guiding them, and they expected Him at any time to establish a new Jewish kingdom and throw out their hated Roman rulers.

Imagine, then, the day Jesus said to them, "By the way, I'm going away—permanently."

Oh, great, the disciples might have thought. *We left everything and were beginning to believe this man, and now the bottom drops out. He's leaving us!*

The events that followed—suspicion, intrigue, torment, and ultimately death on the cross—must have left them dejected, frightened, and altogether puzzled. But the words of Jesus in John 16:7, 12 made the difference: "It is for your good that I am going away. Unless I go away, the Counselor will not come to you; but if I go, I will send him to you. . . . I have much more to say to you, more than you can now bear."

Modern-Day Disciples

My divorce did not affect Christianity for all time to come, and the one who abandoned me was not the Son of God. But I believe the counsel remains the same. I believe that when a door closes in your life, you look for window. I believe that as long as we have someone to depend upon in the natural, we won't totally depend on the One we cannot see. Nevertheless, He will always be there for us—the Counselor, the Comforter, the Holy Spirit.

God has much to teach us, more than we can be taught in the comfortable times of our lives. Our ears open and our arms stretch to receive what God has for us when we are at the end of ourselves.

In the natural, what happened probably never made sense to the disciples. But if we could have a conversation with them today and ask what advice they would give when the bottom drops out, I believe they'd say, "Get down on your knees. While you're picking up the spilled fruit, look up to God. He understands. He made the bucket *and* the fruit, after all. He has much to teach you. Trust us; we know."

❧ ❧ ❧ ❧ ❧ ❧ ❧ ❧

Think about the events that took the bottom out of your bucket. Then answer the following questions:

1. Are you still trying to decide if God is in control—if Jesus is truly the Son of God? Confess your sins before Him. Tell Him you will leave your boat to follow Him no matter what.

2. What do you feel is your greatest loss?

3. What has God taught you on this journey?

"For in the day of trouble he will keep me safe in his dwelling; he will hide me in the shelter of the tabernacle and set me high upon a rock" (Psalm 27:5).

26

Equipping Our Kids
for Relationships

When I was 18, I spent the summer in Arizona, where I dated a man a little older than myself. He had experienced a lot more of life than I had and felt he knew what he wanted; that included getting married. I had just been awarded a one-year scholarship to the university in my hometown, which I considered a great opportunity. I was excited about what the fall would bring, and the last thing I wanted then was to marry.

One night we hiked to the top of a mountain, where we sat and talked. David asked me what my definition of a perfect husband would be. I opened my mouth to respond, but nothing came out. I had never thought about the question. He pressed me for a response.

"Well," I began, "if you asked me for my definition of a perfect mom, I would know. Based on my acquaintance with my own mother, I have some criteria. But until I know someone I want to fit the role of mate in my life, I don't know how to define the perfect husband."

Needless to say, my "romance" with David ended that night. And in the years since, I've often thought of my response—or lack of it. Nine years later, when I married my husband, I had no more idea of what I wanted in a mate than I did that warm Arizona evening with David.

Why We Feel as We Do

Though the reasons vary for why we become single parents, all of us (with the possible exception of the widowed) probably have some degree of regret over the relationship we chose. By looking back on those choices and what motivated them, we can be better equipped for what lies ahead. We need to do that so we won't repeat the same patterns, and our kids need us to do it so they can avoid our mistakes. The process begins by examining the influence of our parents and others in our early years.

As my response to David indicated, what we desire for our adult future comes largely from our growing-up experiences. What did our parents look like? Who made the decisions in everyday affairs? What was the role distinction between Mom and Dad? Research shows that we choose a mate either very similar to or drastically different from our own parent of the opposite sex.

We can't do much about our own early experiences, but we can spare our children some problems. Single-parent kids not only don't see healthy relationships between their moms and dads, but they also don't get the opportunity to learn a balance in parental roles.

My dad was an admirable man in many ways. He pastored a church while continuing his regular vocation. Many respected him and demanded his time. We were unable to participate in many sports activities at school because of our commitments at church 33 miles away. Activities we did join were undertaken without his enthusiasm or affirmation. When I got a modeling job to help put myself through college, for example, Dad criticized me for doing something so senseless.

However, one day, when I went to my dad's place of work to catch a ride, two of the men said, "Are you the one your dad always talks about who is the famous model?" I stood speechless. The guys at work were hearing the words of praise I never got to hear.

Because of my dad's emotional distance, he and I did not develop a relationship in the early years to use as a foundation for the later ones. I grew apathetic toward the fatherly role itself, and that apathy was played out in both the search for and the selection of a husband.

Especially as single parents, we must also be constantly aware of the impact of those people outside the immediate family who touch our children's lives: coaches, relatives, friends, teachers, and even casual acquaintances. Our kids learn from these associations about character, parenting skills, appearance, personality, ambition, chemistry, spirituality, personality, and intelligence. Those individuals contribute either positively or negatively to the kinds of persons our children become and to their ultimate choice of mates.

My first baby-sitting job was for a prominent family in our town. I have many memories from the four years I watched their boys. Most vivid in my mind is the healthy family unit I saw and the affirmation they gave me. They encouraged me to go on to college and even offered to assist me. They motivated me to dream bigger dreams. These and others helped me formulate much of what drives me today.

Do Opposites Attract?

Many times we look for people to fill our empty places or compensate for weaknesses we feel we have. The Bible says we're not to be yoked with unbelievers (see 2 Corinthians 6:14). In part that's because our faith spills over into so many areas of our existence: our thoughts, values, intimacy, interests, beliefs, and expectations about roles, to name just a few.

But even with a fellow believer, there can be critical differences: personal habits, use of money, skills and interests, and variations in values and spiritual beliefs. We should train our children to see these.

What are some major reasons we choose wrong mates in the first place?

• We don't have enough maturity.

• We don't have enough experience.

• One of the individuals involved (maybe both) is too anxious to get married.

• We select a mate to please, or to defy, someone else.

• We don't give ourselves enough time to know potential mates.

• Expectations are unrealistic.

• We ignore behavior or personality problems.

To model good decisions and help our kids make wise choices, we need to find contentment in being single. As we hold ourselves true to God's principles, we will model godly living to our kids and become more content and available to what God has for us now.

Get your whole family involved with people and places that offer unconditional love—church, family, and friends. Find someone to regularly encourage, inspire, listen to, and challenge you, and to hold you accountable.

What to Look for in Love

One summer day, I sat by a pool with a 22-year-old divorced mother of a two-year-old girl.

"I'm seeing someone special," she said. "I'm thinking about moving in with him so we can save money to get married and build a house."

"Is this someone you would like to spend the next 50 years with?" I asked.

"Well . . ." she hesitated. "He's really good to me and my daughter, and he likes to cook. I don't," she added with a smile.

I watched the sunlight dance across the gentle waves on the pool. The little daughter treaded timidly on the steps at the shallow end.

What should this young woman have learned from her failed marriage? What should she know to pass on to her own child? (I'm happy to report that she eventually began attending a nearby church and started making progress toward straightening out her life spiritually and morally.)

Let's teach our kids about the principles we hold dear and the qualities they should search for in friends. Let's equip them with skills that can be carried over into other situations. Above all, let's model daily our devotion to God and let them see us consulting Him for wisdom in decisions both large and small.

I can't change the choices of my youth. But I can make a difference in my kids' futures by equipping them to handle the key issues in selecting a mate.

❧ ❧ ❧ ❧ ❧ ❧ ❧ ❧

1. What are some values your family holds dear?

2. What qualities are important in the friends we select? Why?

3. Name some of the things that have been missing in your relationships. How can you enhance those in your child?

"Do not be yoked together with unbelievers" (2 Corinthians 6:14).

27

Building Upon
the Rock

Family vacations in the West almost every year created an early interest in rocks for me. My uncle, who lived in Arizona, built me a rock
case when I was in sixth grade and mounted and labeled all the important minerals. By the time I worked my way through a geology course
in college, I knew how to find the stuff of which each rock was made.

After I married, I stood beside my husband in church one Sunday
morning. I had grown accustomed to the form and ritual of the service.
But then we sang a song I hadn't heard before. When we got to the
chorus, I knew I would never forget it:

> On Christ the solid rock I stand
> All other ground is sinking sand,
> All other ground is sinking sand.

I remember looking at my unsaved husband. Though raised in a
Christian home, I had never experienced a personal relationship with
Jesus Christ. Now we were building our dream house, so life seemed too
busy for thinking about much else. Starting with the basics of a farm-
house built in 1817, we planned to dig a new foundation and build a
5,500-square-foot home. Along the way, we had to rebuild the old
foundation before we could continue. The work was long and tedious.

Finally, antique hardware graced all the doors, and beveled glass
filtered the rays of the Indiana sun. The original oak floors with square-

head nails were finished to perfection. The whole house was something to behold.

Our first daughter was born, and so was an interest in me to know the things of God. I joined a Bible study, where we studied the book of Matthew. It met mostly in our home, and it was there I read more about rocks:

> Therefore everyone who hears these words of mine and puts them into practice is like a wise man who built his house on the rock. The rain came down, the streams rose, and the winds blew and beat against the house; yet it did not fall, because it had its foundation on the rock. But everyone who hears these words of mine and does not put them into practice is like a foolish man who built his house on sand. The rain came down, the streams rose, and the winds blew and beat against that house, and it fell with a great crash. (Matthew 7:24-27)

I thought about those words as I looked around at everything a woman could want—an exquisite home, paid bills, a healthy child. *Why would anyone choose to waste his time building in the sand?* I thought. *The first wave that comes up makes all his efforts in vain.*

Foundation Problems Again

By the time our second daughter was born, life had become even more busy. Our home was totally finished by then, and we had every reason to enjoy a wonderful life.

Two years later, however, when I was pregnant with our son, I knew something was dreadfully wrong. My husband seemed discontent, and he started leaving our home for lengthy periods. Soon I discovered he was involved with another woman, and the *real* foundation of our home crumbled.

With everything falling apart, I turned to God and truly surrendered my life to Him for the first time. I gave Him all my circumstances and asked Him to build us into a strong family His way.

I finished out the pregnancy and was fearful of what lay ahead. My husband filed for divorce, and 18 months later, it was final.

Building a New Foundation

In the months and years that followed, I found that I couldn't rebuild an old spiritual foundation—it had never really existed. I needed to start from scratch and build anew. That meant, above all, keeping my life pure. Every day, I surrendered to God. I asked Him for guidance and wisdom to make the right decisions. I realized that if sin crept into my life, it would affect all of us, and God's work in and through us would be limited.

But that was only the beginning. Bringing my kids along in the process became of paramount importance. We talked and learned together from Scripture and from the ordinary events of our days. We also became faithfully involved in a nearby church where we were loved and discipled and our talents were used.

One wintry Sunday night, we were driving home from church. On the way, I stopped by the book drop at the library to return some books. And there in the snow were two little kittens. They called loudly to us, and my children begged me to take them home. We had no place to keep them, so I quickly had to decide what else we could do.

I made my way to a fast-food chicken place and asked for some scraps and milk. We came back and fed the kittens, and then we prayed. Seven-year-old Ashley led with "Lord, help someone to take both these babies home tomorrow so they won't have to be split up. And God, show the kittens how to do what's best for them so they won't die."

I promised to call the library in the morning. As we pulled away

Ashley asked, "Mom, did we just help some little angels?"

I did call the library the next day, and I was told an employee had taken both kittens home to her farm. I passed that news on to my children, who witnessed once again God's faithfulness in even the smallest of matters. I knew our foundation was growing strong.

Solid as a Rock

A little later, I sat in our family room and taught my children the Matthew parable, reading them the verses quoted above. I smiled as I thought of the history it holds for me.

"Mom," five-year-old Courtney said, "there's supposed to be an earthquake tomorrow. The teachers are talking about it, and I'm really scared."

With confidence I responded, "Maybe there *will* be an earthquake. If it comes and we die, we're okay. If it doesn't, we're still okay because our home is built on a strong foundation. Right?"

Courtney laughed as I ruffled her hair.

"Now let's get to bed," I said.

Years of fears and problems will follow my children. They'll get into hard places that seem to offer no way out. But today I can say with conviction that my home is built on the Rock. The winds and waves that strike will not take us down. Each of my children is starting to stretch outside the physical boundaries of our house. And I have confidence that the solid bedrock we have found through Jesus Christ will undergird them all along the way.

> On Christ the solid rock we stand,
> All other ground is sinking sand,
> All other ground is sinking sand.

✄ ✄ ✄ ✄ ✄ ✄ ✄ ✄

1. Describe the spiritual foundation of your home. How firm is it?

2. How can you strengthen that foundation? Does it need to be rebuilt or built anew?

3. What's the first step you need to take to make that happen?

"Nevertheless, God's solid foundation stands firm, sealed with this inscription: 'The Lord knows those who are his'" (2 Timothy 2:19).

28

The Scarlet Assurance

When my older daughter started school, I would watch from our bay window each morning as she made her way down the driveway to board the school bus. She would sometimes stop and kick the snow or smell a flower, but she would always scuttle toward that bus and a new day of adventure with enviable, childlike enthusiasm. I would wrap my robe more tightly around me, not knowing what my family would face tomorrow, but sure that today was okay. Her tummy was full of warm oatmeal; her curls with little, yellow bows were still damp from her morning shampoo; and lots of love had hugged her at the door and would be there when she returned.

Yes, she would be all right. I just knew it, even as the Proverbs 31 woman did in a verse I hold dear: "She has no fear for her household; for all of them are clothed in scarlet" (verse 21).

Early Moms and Dads

When God was getting ready to bring Israel out of bondage in Egypt, the last plague He sent because of Pharaoh's resistance was the killing of all the firstborn. As with the earlier plagues, God shielded the Israelite households from the devastation around them. In Exodus 12:7, He commanded the Israelites to smear lamb's blood around the doors of their homes. "When the Lord goes through the land to strike down the Egyptians, he will see the blood on the top and sides of the doorframe and will pass over that doorway, and he will not permit the destroyer to enter your houses and strike you down" (Exodus 12:23). That was, of course, the first Passover.

God went on to instruct Moses that when they entered the land He had promised, they should continue to observe Passover, which included explaining the importance of the event to their children by telling them, "It is the . . . Lord, who passed over the houses of the Israelites in Egypt and spared our homes when he struck down the Egyptians" (Exodus 12:27).

The provision God made for the Israelites was the scarlet blood of the blemish-free sacrificial lamb. And as instructed, moms and dads told this story to their children in the years to come. But during one generation, the story took on a new meaning when Jesus *became* the sacrificial lamb. He was born and lived and then died for us, and His scarlet blood took away the sins from all those who would ask—amid all the devastation around them.

Another Who Found Family Protection

We see other places in the Bible as well where God protected His own from destruction. In Joshua 2, for example, a woman of Jericho named Rahab agreed to do God's bidding and hide two of Joshua's spies. She performed this role after asking for a favor in return—that the Israelites would spare the lives of her family when they conquered the city.

"Our lives for your lives!" the men assured her (Joshua 2:14). They went on to say, "This oath you made us swear will not be binding on us unless, when we enter the land, you have tied this scarlet cord in the window . . . and unless you have brought your father and mother, your brothers and all your family into your house" (Joshua 2:17-18).

Rahab was obedient. She also believed that God was in control and would be faithful to take care of those she loved. She didn't impede

God's ability to work by contemplating her own faults and the wrong decisions she had made. She moved toward her future—helping God's people and ultimately taking her place in the lineage of Christ.

Recently I talked to my teenage daughter about a struggle she was experiencing. Long ago she outgrew her yellow bows, and her little curls have turned to long, brown strands. She still scuttles toward new adventures with enthusiasm. But the challenges have grown more intense with the years. Oatmeal and warm baths are no longer enough to protect her from the dangers that seek to destroy her very soul.

One morning, as we were talking, I again wrapped my robe tightly around me as I said, "If all the roofs of Christian families were painted red, ours would be among the reddest. We've done everything we know to trust Him and live according to His will.

"I believe," I went on to explain, "that God looks down upon those 'red roofs,' pours out His blessings, and, as in the first Passover, blocks destruction from touching the members of those households."

When we listen for God's leading and obey His call, like Moses and Rahab and the virtuous woman of Proverbs 31, He is faithful to care for those we love. We can do only so much. After we've reached those limits, He instructs us to stand firm (see Ephesians 6:13-14).

You're Going the Right Way

Shortly after moving to Colorado, I passed an interstate sign that indicated the exit to Grand Junction, a city on the western edge of the state. *Oh,* I thought, *it's been a long time since I was there. Maybe I'll just buzz over and visit.*

Many months passed before I actually got to Grand Junction. I found out quickly, however, that it wasn't just a "buzz" away, but several hundred miles.

I often think the same way in my spiritual life. I determine I'm on the right road and often expect to get to my destination quickly and without trouble. But the journey seems endless and difficult at times, and it causes me to miss the beauty along the way. Sometimes I doubt that I'm the best person to make the journey or that I'm even heading in the right direction.

But if we're following Christ and His map and doing our best for Him, we're on the right road. With the scarlet cord of God's provision in our windows, whatever our families need will be supplied. This may not always happen in the way or the timing we would expect, and we may have to learn the difference between what we *need* and what we *want*. Nonetheless, when we follow Him by faith, we *will* find Him faithful.

❧ ❧ ❧ ❧ ❧ ❧ ❧ ❧

Just for fun, look back on the journey you've made so far as a single parent:

Where and when did you start?

How did you feel at the time?

Which way did you proceed?

How did you know to go in that direction?

What were some of the things that scared you along the way?

Name the troubles you encountered.

Describe the "scenery" you saw.

What were the places along the road where you found God faithful?

Were you able to help someone else on the way?

How has the journey been worth the effort?

As you look ahead, how do you feel? Is there anything that causes you concern?

How can you cover your family with scarlet for the miles that lie in front of you?

Now continue on your journey. You're on the right road. You're the best man—or woman—for the job. Consult your map (your Bible) often, and sing away your fears.

"When it snows, she has no fear for her household; for all of them are clothed in scarlet" (Proverbs 31:21).

29

Taking His Lead

Some days I grow weary of both the small inconveniences and the big decisions that fill my life. I wonder, *What if I make a wrong choice that messes up my family?* When I have one of those days, I try to find a quiet place and remind myself who I am in Christ. Psalm 23 helps me.

Old Words, Fresh Meaning

In this familiar psalm, David wrote from the perspective of a sheep, and the first verse sets the mood for the entire chapter: "The Lord is my shepherd, I shall not be in want."

A flock has many sheep but just one shepherd, and each sheep knows the shepherd's voice. Some shepherds give names to their sheep, and the sheep respond when they're called. "The sheep listen to his voice. He calls his own sheep by name and leads them out" (John 10:3).

A good shepherd takes his flock to nourishing grass and water and protects them from danger. The sheep don't have to worry about anything, such as taking wrong paths.

"He makes me lie down in green pastures" (verse 2).

Sheep are not smart animals. They lack common sense and are defenseless.

One day when my son was in kindergarten, we were walking along a sidewalk, identifying flowers and shrubs. We came to a holly bush, and I picked one of its leaves. I touched a sharp point to Clint's arm and told him that the holly leaf uses those sharp edges to protect itself.

He peered at the leaf curiously as we walked to the car. I started the engine. Suddenly he unfastened his seatbelt, stood from the backseat, and held the leaf proudly before him as he said, "Mommy, if someone tries to break into our car, we'll be okay. I'll protect us with my holly leaf."

For the next two hours, he asked me how every animal he could think of protected itself. Rabbits run, snakes bite, and cats climb trees. But what could I tell him about lambs? They have awkward hooves and spindly legs. They have no natural source of protection.

Sheep are also fearful. Sudden, unfamiliar noises cause them to stampede and blindly follow each other. When one gets nervous, therefore, the shepherd squeezes its ear, which is very sensitive, and forces its head down to graze and rest in green pastures.

"He leads me beside quiet waters. He restores my soul" (verses 2-3).

Sheep don't like fast currents or rushing water. They're poor swimmers, and if their wool gets soaked, they sink. The shepherd collects stones from the banks of a stream and dams the water to form still pools. Then the sheep can drink in a calm setting.

Stubborn lambs, however, are sometimes determined to go their own way. Isaiah drew on this image when he wrote, "We all, like sheep, have gone astray, each of us has turned to his own way" (Isaiah 53:6). When sheep wander, the shepherd restores them. "To restore" means to bring back to a previous or original condition—convincing a willful sheep to turn around to follow the shepherd once again. Its inward bent has been changed.

Sometimes sheep get themselves into dangerous places and call loudly to their shepherd. The shepherd runs to their aid, and with his staff he pulls them to safety. If a lamb continues to go its own way, the shepherd will hit it on the leg, causing a break. He cleans and sets the wound, then carries the lamb until it is restored.

When the lamb is walking on its own once again, it sticks close to the shepherd. The discipline hurt, and the memory is sharp when the lamb has the urge to wander again. "No discipline seems pleasant at the time, but painful. Later on, however, it produces a harvest of righteousness and peace for those who have been trained by it" (Hebrews 12:11).

"He guides me in paths of righteousness for his name's sake" (verse 3).

Before my family goes into a restaurant or for a visit with friends, I remind my children to demonstrate good manners. Why? For my name's sake. I'll look good if they look good.

The shepherd, who has much invested in his flock, leads the sheep carefully down the right paths, not just for the sheep's sake, but also for his own. Sheep's wool is the shepherd's source of profit; dead sheep grow no wool.

When skiing in the Big Burn area of Aspen, Colorado, while I was still married, my husband always led the way because he was familiar with the trails. As long as he was in the lead, I arrived safely. One day, however, I felt overly confident in my modest abilities and moved into the lead. I was either too busy to notice or too stupid to care that I had entered an area clearly marked for advanced skiers.

I shooshed down, carving through moguls as if I knew what I was doing. Halfway down the slope, I turned around to find my husband still standing at the mouth of the trail we were *supposed* to take. I examined the treacherous path I had just descended and then turned to look at the even more treacherous one between me and the bottom of the trail. I stopped and began calling for help. He came and led me down to safety.

"Even though I walk through the valley of the shadow of death, I will fear no evil, for you are with me; your rod and your staff, they comfort me" (verse 4).

One February night when my children were young, I put them to bed at their regular time. Then I cleaned my house from top to bottom; baked a birthday cake; decorated the basement with streamers, balloons, and signs; wrapped presents; and prepared lunch for the following day. I got no sleep that night, and I was just finishing the preparations when the children awoke the next morning. My daughter rubbed her eyes and asked, "What's for breakfast?" She had slept peacefully while I provided everything she needed for her party that day.

The shepherd may have to make many arrangements or slay innumerable enemies, but the sheep's sleep is sweet. The sheep accepts its own helplessness and knows it will always need the help of the shepherd.

The journey, however, is often rugged. Severe winters and quick thaws can cause dangerous changes in the terrain. Deep ravines make for unsure footing. At these times, the sheep draw in particularly close to the shepherd, who uses certain instruments to assist in his leading. The *rod* is a club fashioned by weaving pieces of bone into oak limbs. It serves as a weapon to protect the sheep. The *staff* is used in guiding. With these two pieces of equipment, the shepherd has everything under control.

Likewise we can say, even in difficult circumstances, "I will lie down and sleep in peace, for you alone, O Lord, make me dwell in safety" (Psalm 4:8).

"You prepare a table before me in the presence of my enemies. You anoint my head with oil; my cup overflows" (verse 5).

Small snakes sometimes bite the noses and necks of grazing sheep. So the shepherd spreads a pungent oil around snake holes in his pasture and upon the noses and necks of his sheep. He anoints their heads with oil to protect them from the enemy. He also fills to overflowing small containers of fresh water for the sheep to drink.

"Surely goodness and love will follow me all the days of my life, and I will dwell in the house of the Lord forever" (verse 6).

What does this psalm mean to you and me? Just like the sheep, you and I must remember that we are not the shepherd—only one of His flock. We can't fight our own battles, call our own shots, or choose our own paths without getting into grave difficulty. Every detail of our lives must be surrendered daily to the Great Shepherd's wisdom. I am learning to accept my own ignorance and inability and allow Him to lead. When my ineptness is willingly exchanged for His complete sufficiency, I watch as goodness and mercy follow me.

In Joe Bayly's poem *Psalm of Wandering,* he captured the resolve of the sheep to be led by the shepherd. Because of the sheep's own inadequacies, the sufficiency of the shepherd comes through.

> Lord you know
> I'm such a stupid sheep.
> I worry
> about all sorts of things.
> Whether I'll find grazing land
> still cool water
> a fold at night

in which I can feel safe.
I don't.
I only find troubles
want
loss.
I turn aside from You
to plan my rebel way.
I go astray.
I follow other shepherds
even other stupid sheep.
Then when I end up
on some dark mountain cliffs before
wild animals behind
I start to bleat
Shepherd, Shepherd
find me save me
or I die.
And you do.

(From Psalms of My Life, *Chariot Victor Publishing, copyright 1987. Used by permission of Chariot Victor Publishing.)*

❇ ❇ ❇ ❇ ❇ ❇ ❇ ❇

Make this prayer your own:

Dear Shepherd:
Thank You for this reminder. Help me remember that I don't have to be in want. Remind me to lie down and trust in Your sufficiency and control. Teach me how to follow Your leading. And help me and my family to dwell in the house of the Lord forever. Amen.

"The Lord is my shepherd, I shall not be in want" (Psalm 23:1).

30

To Know Him

The Bible says in Daniel 11:32, "The people that do know their God shall be strong and do exploits" (KJV). The word *know* in this passage comes from the Hebrew word *yada*. It means "life-giving intimacy," and it can be found in scriptures like Genesis 4:1: "And Adam *knew* Eve his wife; and she conceived, and bare Cain" (KJV).

Another biblical character, Mary of Bethany, also confronted the meaning of *yada*. I sometimes imagine what it might have been like for her to learn this intimacy with her Lord. What follows is my attempt to re-create that scene.

The Good Part

The streets of Bethany were busy. Everyone was preparing for the Feast of the Passover and Unleavened Bread—just two days away. Mary stopped by the market, where she heard two men talking. "The chief priests and scribes are trying to find a way to kill him," one said. "I hear they'll wait till the festival is over, as I'm sure there will be a riot."

"Yes," replied the other. "Surely this will be the end of Jesus of Nazareth."

The words stabbed Mary's heart like a knife as she repeated, "Jesus of Nazareth?"

She dropped the fruit she had been inspecting and ran home as fast as she could. The words "Jesus of Nazareth" seemed to pound with her steps on the street.

Mary rushed into her house. All was quiet. She and her family had been invited for supper at the home of Simon. Mary's sister, Martha, had gone ahead to help serve. Mary thought about Jesus and the times He had sat with them in this very house.

She walked to a chair and knelt down before it as she had done with Jesus. His words warmed her heart as she remembered learning at His feet. Martha had once complained to Jesus that Mary wasn't helping to prepare a meal. But Jesus had replied, "This thing is needful. Mary has chosen that good part, which shall not be taken away from her."

Mary smiled until she recalled the frightening words of the men in the marketplace. She stood, pulled her shawl around her, and walked toward the room of her brother, Lazarus, whom Jesus raised from the dead.

Mary sat on the edge of the bed. She remembered when her brother was sick, how they had sent for Jesus, saying, "Lord, the one you love is sick."

But Jesus did not come for two days, and Lazarus had died and was buried. Many people had come to comfort the sisters. Then someone had announced that Jesus was on His way. Martha had risen, gone out to meet Him, and returned shortly, saying, "The Teacher is asking for you."

Mary had gone out to Him as others followed. When she saw Jesus, she fell at His feet and said, "Lord, if you had been here, my brother would not have died."

Then Mary and those around her had cried. She looked up into the face of Jesus and saw His eyes were also full of tears. "Where have you laid him?" Jesus had asked.

He had walked toward the tomb and commanded that the stone be removed from the entrance. He had looked up and prayed, "Father, I thank you that you have heard me. I knew that you always hear me, but I said this for the benefit of the people standing here, that they may believe that you sent me." Then He called in a loud voice, "Lazarus, come out!"

And Lazarus had risen and walked out of the tomb.

Mary stood, snapping out of her reverie. *Why do they want to kill Jesus?* she wondered. *What can I do? How can I show Him how much I care?* And then she remembered that the greatest ritual she could perform on such royalty as the Son of God was to anoint Him.

Mary moved swiftly to her room and gathered her alabaster box of expensive pure nard. She clutched it to her breast as she made her way to the home of Simon. She thought about the perfume made from the dried leaves of the rare grass from India that lay inside the box. She knew its value could be put to many good purposes. But she quickened her steps toward her Master.

Mary stopped at the door of Simon's house. She hesitated, took a deep breath, and tightened her hold on the alabaster box. She pushed the door open and walked inside. The men were reclining around the table. Martha stopped serving and looked at her sister. No one spoke.

Mary walked to Jesus. She broke the seal of the alabaster box, turned it up, and poured perfume on His head and clothes. Then she stooped and anointed His feet with the perfume and wiped them with her hair. The house was filled with its fragrance.

Judas asked, "Why has there been such a waste? This perfume could have been sold for much and given to the poor."

But Jesus said, "You have the poor with you always, me you do not. She has anointed me for my burial."

Mary and the others watched Jesus for the next two days. The scent of the perfume Mary poured on Him out of her undying devotion went with Him toward the Passover, the Garden of Gethsemane, Herod's hall, and Pilate's palace. Finally, Jesus was beaten, spit upon, and hung on the cross at Calvary.

Mary looked on in despair. She cried as she realized her Lord had been killed. But then she remembered His words: "Mary has chosen the good part, which shall not be taken away from her."

Mary pulled this pledge close and, with new hope in her heart, turned and walked away.

What Kind of Love Is This?

When I was a child, my heart was full of love. I loved my parents, "Mr. Ed," and peanut-butter-and-jelly sandwiches. I loved loving and being loved. I matured into a world that spoke much of love. The TV talked about it, books esteemed it, and people sought it. So I began my search for a love of my own. I sank it into intangibles—my education and career. But when the degree was earned and the job became routine, I realized how fruitless my search had turned.

When I found a person on whom I could lavish the love I felt, I poured it on him like honey. My days and plans and efforts were devoted to him. And then he was gone. Did true love really exist?

When I found Christ, I found One who loved me just as I was, all the time, in every way. No matter what I did or how I felt, I couldn't lessen His love for me. But I still needed someone for *me* to love. I couldn't see *Him*. I couldn't touch Him. My search was still on.

More troubles came. They hurt as before, but *unlike* the past, I now felt Someone was going through these difficulties with me. Every day that passed and in every way, I felt Him draw close to me, and I knew Him more. I talked to Him about what was happening and read about Him in His Word. He listened to me, He helped me, and He loved me. And then I realized that I loved Him, too.

Has He ever left me? Never. Has He remained a constant companion? Always. My relationship with God—as it did for Mary—has grown out of the tough times when there was no one else. You and I as single parents are not more needy than other members of our church congregations. We just live lives that are stripped of the pretense that we can do it alone. This realization offers us the greatest opportunity to really get to know the One who "will never leave us or forsake us."

Our streets and neighborhoods and even our churches contain individuals whose lives have turned out as they planned in many ways—yet they feel empty. For without that intimate fellowship with God, they are often still alone.

Now is the time to make a difference for ourselves and those around us. To "be strong and do mighty exploits" inside and outside our homes, we must intimately know our God. The more we become acquainted with Him, the stronger we are to handle what we face. We can choose many different paths and priorities, but like Mary, we need to choose the good part. That good part means sitting at the feet of Jesus. It means giving our hurts and tears to the One who cares. It means taking time to listen to what He's saying to us. It means becoming strong in His strength. These are the things that can never be taken away.

❧ ❧ ❧ ❧ ❧ ❧ ❧ ❧

1. Think about your best friend. How did that relationship evolve? It may have begun with a formal introduction. Have you formally met Christ? Take the time to do so. Tell Him who you are and how much you want to be acquainted with Him and have your sins forgiven.

2. Once you've met Him, you need to cultivate that friendship. How might you do that?

• By talking to Him every day about everything.

• By reading all you can about Him in His Word.

• By relating to others who also have an intimate relationship with Him.

• By letting Him know how much you love Him.

• By singing His praises.

• By sharing this intense love for Him with others—especially your children.

"I want to know Christ and the power of his resurrection" (Philippians 3:10).

31

Capture the Teachable Moments

The best opportunities to teach my children important life lessons come at unexpected times. Each presents a brief window of opportunity for learning, and I try desperately to make the most of it.

Through the years, God has helped me develop some creative lessons. I was able to illustrate the brevity of life in the roses we picked one day after the death of the kids' great-grandfather. A bird's nest helped us understand the importance of good parenting. The need for freezing temperatures to enhance the quality of maple syrup helped us recognize the reasons for hard times.

One day my children returned from children's church talking about the fruit of the Spirit found in Galatians 5:22-23. I captured the moment by writing stories they could understand and revisit when their own times of Christian development were right. And that's when they met Molly and Luke.

The Fruit

Molly opened her eyes, and the clock told her she had overslept. She pulled back the quilt Grandmother had made and swung her feet to the side. The cold wooden floor made her toes curl on this spring morning, and she longed to pull them up again to the warmth of her bed.

Molly stuffed her gown into her dresser drawer, closing it on part of the white lace. She put on her red sweater, jeans, and tennis shoes, and down the steps she ran, two at a time.

"Hold up there, young lady," said Mom. "Where are you going so fast?"

"Today is pruning day. We get to help Dad in the orchard," Molly said, reaching for her jacket.

"After you eat and make your bed, you can catch up," insisted Mom, whose stern look told Molly an argument would do no good.

Molly sat down, said a prayer, and cut the butter into the steamy bowl of oatmeal on the table. As she began to eat, the fresh maple syrup she had added dripped down her chin, and she savored its sweetness.

When breakfast and chores were finished, Molly kissed her mom good-bye. She pushed open the squeaky screen door and stepped outside. Mom handed her warm biscuits with honey and said, "Tell your dad lunch will be ready at noon."

"Okay, Mom," said Molly over her shoulder as she swept across the yard toward the orchard. She spotted Dad's blue pickup truck and scooted toward it.

Dad was leaning on his long ladder with his shears. He caught a glimpse of Molly and smiled at her through the branches. "Morning, Mol," he said.

"Mom sent some biscuits," Molly said as brother Luke took his hands from his pockets and stretched them toward his sister. Dad climbed down from the ladder. He chewed his biscuit and ruffled Molly's hair as he surveyed the tree.

"You know," he said, "this old tree has given us lots of fruit. But it wouldn't be so good if someone hadn't cut back the limbs that don't make it through the winter."

"What happened to this branch?" Luke asked. "It's hanging from the tree, but its leaves and buds are all shriveled up."

"Son, the branch can't bear fruit by itself," Dad said. "It must be completely attached to the tree. If that connection is broken, its leaves and fruit dry up." He reached out, cut off the branch, and threw it onto the pile to be burned.

"Look at this good branch," said Molly. "It's loaded with buds."

"Not a good branch," Dad said, "a good tree. This old tree has strong roots that give food and water to the branches. The glory of the fruit goes to the tree, not the branch. Speaking of trees, let's get back to work."

It was a little past noon when Dad, Molly, and Luke headed home for lunch. By the back door, Dad stopped, reached up, and picked a small branch from a redbud tree. As they sat down to eat, Molly and Luke watched as Dad set the redbud bouquet in the center of the table. He also placed a wilted daffodil and hyacinth there.

Molly and Luke snickered. "Those are lovely, Dad," Luke said.

"Yes," said Dad, smiling. "All these flowers were cut from the main plant. This daffodil was cut one week ago, this hyacinth one day ago, and these redbud flowers just a minute ago. This one is about gone, this one is just beginning to wilt, and this one still looks pretty good.

"But the fact is, they're all dying. As long as they remained a part of the plant, they grew and blossomed. The moment they were cut from the plant, however, their death began. They're all in different phases of that death, but it will surely come to all of them.

"Molly, Luke," Dad went on, "our relationship with God is the same way. If we stay close to our heavenly Father and live according to His principles, we'll grow and be strong. We'll even begin to look like the main 'tree' of which we're a part. If any of us should decide we don't need the tree anymore, however, and we allow something or someone to cut us off, spiritual death will surely come. It may not happen within the hour or day or week. But it will happen."

"How can we start looking like God the way the daffodil looks like the plant and the branches look like the apple tree?" Molly asked.

"By growing fruit," Dad answered.

"I know how to eat fruit like apples and oranges," Luke said. "But I don't know how to grow them. What is the fruit in our lives supposed to be?"

Mom handed Dad a Bible. He opened it and read, "But the fruit of the Spirit is love, joy, peace, patience, kindness, goodness, faithfulness, gentleness and self-control" (Galatians 5:22).

"That's a lot of fruit, Dad," said Luke. "I don't even know what some of that means. Am I supposed to grow *all* that fruit?"

"Son, as you grow one kind, God uses that to help feed someone else. Then God helps you grow another kind. He will grow all of them in you when it's time."

Lunch was finished. Molly, Luke, and Dad went back out the door. They stopped briefly by the old tire swing. Dad pushed Molly while Luke chased a butterfly across the yard. The spring breeze felt fresh in Molly's face as Dad grabbed the ropes and pulled the swing to a halt. Then Dad put on his gloves and said, "It's time for us to get to work. I hear our fall crop calling." And off they went.

The Fruits of My Labors

Several years have passed since I wrote that story for my kids. But today, each of them can tell you who Molly and Luke are. More importantly, they can tell you about the fruit they each learned about through additional stories we wrote together—about issues like love and joy and peace—that made sense in their everyday lives.

The stories aren't so remarkable. Nor are the lessons they convey. What I hope you'll remember here is that this mom did her best to capture a moment with her kids when the time was right to hone in on a biblical truth.

I believe these moments lie all along the paths we walk, in comments made by friends and through the tough circumstances that confront us. We must tune our ears to hear them. They speak to us through the mouths of those whose hands we hold. They speak to us through the mouth of God. Let's learn to hear. Let's learn to stop and follow through. Let's learn to share them with our kids. One day we'll be the grandparents watching our children pass God's truth on to their kids.

❧ ❧ ❧ ❧ ❧ ❧ ❧ ❧

Describe some of the teachable moments you've had with your kids.

What happened?

What did your children learn?

How does that affect them today?

How can you capture more teachable moments?

"These commandments that I give you today are to be upon your hearts. Impress them on your children. Talk about them when you sit at home and when you walk along the road, when you lie down and when you get up" (Deuteronomy 6:6-7).

32

Strengthening the Lines of Defense

"Red rover, red rover. We dare Lynda over."
Remember that schoolyard game from your elementary years? (Maybe you're not as old as I am!) Two teams would line up facing each other, with hands joined. Then someone would call a name from the other side, and that person would run across and try to break through the opposing team's line. If the individual succeeded, he was permitted to take one person back with him to his own team. If not, he had to stay.

I remember well the strategy I would use when my name was called. My eyes would search the opposing team and select what I thought was the most vulnerable place in its line. Then, with all the speed, determination, and strength I could muster, I would shoot across the field and slice between my victims.

The Weak Link

I read of three characters in the Bible who probably knew what it felt like to be the losing team in red rover. They all had their act together in many ways, yet one vulnerable place in their "lines" permitted an opponent to break through.

Solomon was the wisest man who ever lived and was greatly blessed by God. "Solomon showed his love for the Lord by walking according to the statutes of his father David, *except* that he offered sacrifices and burned incense on the high places" (1 Kings 3:3, emphasis added). When Solomon failed to surrender this weakness to God, it proved to be his undoing in spite of his great wisdom.

David, Solomon's father, was spoken of as a man after God's own heart (see 1 Samuel 13:14). Yet one great weakness he failed to surrender to God was his desire for a married woman. He gave in to that lust, and the sin affected not only his life, but also the lives of his family and nation for generations to follow.

Samson was a miraculous gift to a barren mother. An angel appeared to her and said, "You are sterile and childless, but you are going to conceive and have a son. . . . set apart to God from birth, and he will begin a deliverance of Israel from the hands of the Philistines" (Judges 13:3, 5).

And he did. "He grew and the Lord blessed him, and the spirit of the Lord began to stir him while he was in Mahaneh Dan" (Judges 13:24-25). But Samson had a weakness for Philistine women, and he pursued them, ignoring his father's warnings. This cost him his strength and, ultimately, his life.

Then there was the rich young ruler who came up to Jesus and asked, "Teacher, what good thing must I do to get eternal life?" (Matthew 19:16).

Jesus explained to him that he had to obey the commandments of God.

At that point, I'm sure this red-rover-playing young ruler must have examined the "line" of his life and seen all its strong junctures. He responded to Jesus, "All these have I kept."

But then he asked Jesus a question that I believe you and I must ask today: "In spite of all the things I am doing right, what do I still lack?"

Of course, Jesus saw clearly the weakest point in the young man's devotion to God—his love of wealth. Jesus simply said, "If you want to be perfect, go, sell your possessions and give to the poor, and you will have treasure in heaven. Then come, follow me" (Matthew 19:21).

What was Jesus asking? He was asking this young man to wade into deeper waters with Him. He was giving him the choice of playing with his commitment or going all out to follow God. He was asking the young man for a deliberate decision to exchange his *things* for eternal service to the kingdom of God.

What decision did the man make? "When the young man heard this, he went away sad, because he had great wealth" (Matthew 19:22). He walked away from Christ.

Missionary Jim Eliot rightly said that a man is no fool to give up what he can't keep in order to gain what he can never lose. But by that definition, this young man was the worst kind of fool.

Looking Within

In the busy lives we lead—at work, home, and church—we encounter conflict and hardship. It's easy to look at our co-workers, family members, or people within our congregations and determine what they're doing wrong. Recently, however, God has been teaching me to look *within myself* to find what might be going wrong in the situations and relationships around me. Have I failed to forgive the one who brought me harm? Do I say unkind words about those who believe differently from me? Am I falling short in the love department and overflowing with impatience toward those who don't believe in Christ?

I believe that life's spiritual battlefields are dotted with fellow Christians—potentially great men and women of God—who failed to surrender their weak points to God, and it became their downfall.

Early in the Bible, God told Moses that when Israel got into the Promised Land, they were to destroy all the inhabitants, or those nations would forever cause Israel problems (see Numbers 33:55). One passage in Joshua shows what happened when they failed to carry out that command. Some men from the city of Gibeon tricked them into believing they were from a far-off land. Joshua and his men did not consult God and fell for the ruse. So they ate with the men of Gibeon, which established a new covenant between the two nations. And from that point on in Jewish history, the Gibeonites did not go away but remained trouble to Israel always.

The principle for us is that as we move forward with God, we can't let old sins remain. Our "lines" will not remain impenetrable unless each and every joint is secure. We must look to God daily to reinforce those lines—to help us resist temptation and make right choices. After all, we're constantly being attacked by people and circumstances that seek to defeat us.

The way I do this is to go to God in prayer and lay out who I am and what I'm facing. I also listen—to His Word and to His Spirit in prayer—and allow Him to fill me with wisdom and reveal the weaknesses in my defense. Then throughout the day, I become aware of ways in which I'm not being quite honest with myself or others, or I'm giving responses that don't display the long-suffering of Christ.

One morning, God made me aware of how poorly I was responding to my daughters' unsaved friends. He let me know that He loved them as much as He loved my own children. Yet in my arrogance, I had sought only to save *my* children and to make the best decisions for them. I realized I hadn't even been praying that God would touch their lives.

Solomon, David, and Samson failed to surrender their weak points before they did them in. The rich young ruler had the right intentions but lacked the resolve to turn all else loose and serve God unreservedly. As Corrie ten Boom once said, "Hold everything loosely. It hurts when God has to pry your fingers loose."

God wants people who will stand firm and strong for Him and will go to any lengths throughout their lives to do that job better. He wants the hearts of people who never feel as if they've arrived. He wants those who stay moldable and ready to do His bidding no matter what the cost.

"This one thing you lack," say the words of God to us today. He wants us to listen, lock arms, and dig our feet down firmly into the ground. We and God are an unbeatable team. But we must listen to the Coach if we're going to win the game.

❦ ❦ ❦ ❦ ❦ ❦ ❦ ❦

This week, may I challenge you to get quiet before God each day with your Bible and your journal? Ask Him to tell you where you're weak. Then do the following:

1. Listen carefully to what He speaks to your heart.

2. Write it down with today's date.

3. Ask for His forgiveness if you've sinned in that area, and for guidance in growing stronger in Him. You might also need to ask God to forgive you for hurting others.

4. Thank God for His faithfulness and sufficiency. Go about your day. Take on any opponent you must. Then come back to Him afresh about your battle plan for the new day.

"What do I still lack?" (Matthew 19:20).

33

The Call.
It's for You.

One afternoon when my son, Clint, was in kindergarten, he returned home from school and asked me to read him a story. I was preparing for a class I would teach that night, but I stopped to read to him on our family room couch.

He chose the Bible story about Hannah and Samuel from one of his books. I related the familiar story to him, as well as the actual account from 1 Samuel. Then I stopped and said, "In chapter 1, Samuel's mother blessed him. In chapter 2, he was smiled on by God and man. But in chapter 3, the Bible says Samuel didn't know God until he received the call of God himself."

I looked Clint in the eye as I said, "Hannah and I have a lot in common. We both prayed for a son, and God looked all over heaven and gave us the best He had. You've been blessed by me since before you were born. God and man have smiled on you, but you must decide for yourself whether your life will belong to Him."

I pointed to our fireplace and continued, "At one time, that fireplace was just a big pile of bricks. Then the pile was given to someone with skill. He built it into something of beauty using the whole bricks as well as the chipped and broken ones.

In a similar way, you must choose whether you'll give all your bricks—the broken, chipped, and whole ones—to God regardless of how much you've been blessed by everyone else. God will decide what He'll make out of them."

My Call to the Call

Describing Samuel's call from God to Clint made me interested in others in the Bible who also received divine calls. So I started looking and found several. Here are just a few:

Abram was a wealthy man who lived with his barren wife in Haran. The call came to him in Genesis 12:1: "Leave your country, your people and your father's household and go to the land I will show you." Abram's response? "So Abram left, as the Lord had told him" (Genesis 12:4).

Moses was brought up by the Pharaoh's daughter. He killed an Egyptian and fled to Midian for his life. He married there and kept his father-in-law's flock. Then one day, "God called to him from within the bush, 'Moses! Moses!' And Moses said, 'Here I am'" (Exodus 3:4).

Jeremiah lived during some dark days in Judah caused by the disobedience of the Israelites. His call is recorded in Jeremiah 1:5-6: "Before I formed you in the womb I knew you, before you were born I set you apart; I appointed you as a prophet to the nations." Jeremiah responded with these words: "Ah, Sovereign Lord, . . . I do not know how to speak; I am only a child." Then Jeremiah obeyed.

Isaiah didn't directly hear the call of God. He just heard God asking, "Whom shall I send? And who will go for us?" Isaiah responded, "Here I am. Send me" (Isaiah 6:8).

What Message Did the Caller Leave?

Webster's dictionary defines *call* as: "to name, select, appoint or designate for an office, duty or employment." How does God accomplish that?

• *God calls different kinds of people to do different kinds of work.* Abram was rich, but Gideon was poor. Moses was old, but Jeremiah, David, and Samuel were young. Paul was single, but others were married. Among these individuals were prophets, teachers, priests, writers, and kings. God's call is not just for a special few, but only a few hear it. Isaiah just overheard God asking, "Who will go?"

• *God uses many things to get the attention of those He calls.* He used an angel with Gideon, a light from heaven with Paul, and a burning bush with Moses. God also calls us quietly out of the ordinary or even the tragic events of our lives, like my divorce.

• *God meets us where we are and asks for what we have.* David was on a hillside guarding sheep. Samuel was in bed. Paul was on the road to persecute God's people. Gideon was threshing wheat by the winepress. Joshua was wandering in the wilderness. Moses was on the back side of the desert. God requires from us only what we have. He asked for a boy's fishes and loaves, not hamburgers and french fries that he didn't have.

• *The extent of the call varies.* The primary call of God is not to any particular service but to devotion to Jesus Christ. To serve God is the deliberate love gift of a nature that has heard the call. We serve Him in ordinary ways out of our devotion. The passion of Paul's life was to proclaim the gospel of Jesus. He welcomed heartbreaks, disillusionment, and tribulations for one reason—to follow the call.

• *The responses to the call vary.* Gideon questioned, made excuses, asked for a sign, and then obeyed. Paul fell to the earth in immediate conversion. Jonah refused to answer in the beginning, and then he obeyed. Abram (Abraham) faltered by getting ahead of God.

• *The call of God is only the beginning.* To be devoted to the gospel means to nip ambitions, quench desires, and extinguish outlooks that would pull us in other directions. The call of God makes us never the same again. Once we have received a commission from God, we're no longer content to work for Him halfheartedly.

• *The call of God asks only for obedience.* God is not working toward a particular finish the way we often do. The boy with the fishes and loaves saw immediate results. But David went back home, tended his sheep faithfully, and waited to take his place in the call. Several years passed between Paul's conversion and the beginning of his ministry. What we see as the process, God sees as the end. His call starts now. It doesn't begin when we reach a certain level, like David becoming king of Israel. It starts in the shepherd's field and continues with being obedient in the everyday things. If we have a further end in view, we don't pay sufficient attention to the immediate and may miss God's direction. Obedience is the end.

Call Waiting

I get frustrated when I'm talking to someone on the phone and she says, "I have to go. I'm getting another call."

That message implies, *Maybe this caller is more important than you. Hold on. I'll get back to you after I check this out.*

I fear, however, that sometimes we do the same thing with the call of God. When He summons us to work for Him, we tend to say, "Hold on, Lord. I have another call I want to check out. Perhaps this other one is more important or more to my liking."

My personal call to duty came when my husband left me pregnant and the mother of one- and three-year-old daughters. Not knowing what to do, I cried out to God for help. I heard His call one night when I found 1 Chronicles 28:10: "Consider now, for the Lord has chosen you to build a temple as a sanctuary. Be strong and do the work." He chose me to raise my children for Him. And regardless of what else has been piled on my plate since then, that call has remained the same through the years.

God wants us first to be available to hear the call, then to accept it without reservation. He wants us to do as Elisha did—kill our oxen and burn our plows behind us (see 1 Kings 19:21). That leaves us nothing to go back to.

Where will God's call take us? None of us knows. "By faith Abraham, when called to go to a place he would later receive as his inheritance, obeyed and went, even though he did not know where he was going. . . . For he was looking forward to the city with foundations, whose architect and builder is God" (Hebrews 11:8, 10).

God is calling to you and me today, "Who will go for Me?" You and I need to hear that call and respond with, "Here I am." That response will change everything—for us and our children.

The call. It's for you.

❊ ❊ ❊ ❊ ❊ ❊ ❊ ❊

1. Has God placed a call on your life? Describe it.

2. When did it occur?

3. How did it change you?

4. What can you do to recommit to the call?

"For many are invited; but few are chosen" (Matthew 22:14).

34

True Importance

We live in a society that often evaluates people in vocational and financial terms. Our role models—the people who count the most—are the ones with prestigious jobs and big incomes.

As single parents, we often feel as if we're at the bottom of the heap. Others have more clout, contribute larger amounts of money, and are missed more in their absence. In the church as well as the neighborhood, we feel as if we're the only ones who stand alone. And we often think, *What do I bring to the Body of Christ except a background full of regrets?*

Whenever I'm tempted to think that way, God sends me a reminder of how essential are *all* the ingredients in any endeavor. I wasn't able to finish the waffles I began the other morning until my daughter borrowed from our neighbor the cup of oil we were missing. We also put a puzzle together recently, only to find a piece missing. Not until one of my children found it later were we able to complete the picture. Which one of the pieces was the most important?

Who Was the Greatest?

Since childhood, I've heard the story of Saul's conversion:

Meanwhile, Saul was still breathing out murderous threats against the Lord's disciples . . . so that if he found any there who belonged to the Way, whether men or women, he

might take them as prisoners to Jerusalem. As he
neared Damascus on his journey, suddenly a light from
heaven flashed around him. He fell to the ground and
heard a voice say to him, "Saul, Saul, why do you persecute me?" (Acts 9:1-4)

His conversion at that moment changed the course of history
and led to his authorship of much of the New Testament. But in a
way, his conversion began long before his Damascus road experience, with the people who for years went to their deaths witness-
ing to this man about Christ. Were these unnamed martyrs of the
faith among the greatest?

The same Paul wrote his epistle to the Romans while in
Macedonia. He was busy there and couldn't deliver it personally.
So in the absence of fax machines or Federal Express, he asked
someone to deliver it for him. It may well have been a woman
named Phoebe, about whom he wrote, "I commend to you our
sister Phoebe, a servant of the church in Cenchrea. I ask you to
receive her in the Lord in a way worthy of the saints and to give her
any help she may need from you, for she has been a great help to
many people, including me" (Romans 16:1-2).

Who was the greater, Paul who wrote the words or the person
who delivered them? Both were essential if God's message was
going to reach Rome.

I have a friend named Susan who witnessed for 12 years to an
atheist friend. The friend, Nancy, seemed to pay no heed. One day,
however, Susan called me with excitement in her voice. "Guess
what," she said. "A perfect stranger just led Nancy to the Lord. Can
you believe it?" Who was the greater, Susan or the woman who
actually prayed the sinner's prayer with Nancy?

Another friend of mine, Jerry, visited a church where he didn't know anyone. A newly single dad, Jerry was still reeling from a divorce that left him feeling rejected, depressed, and alone. As Jerry walked from his car to the church's door, a man directing cars in the parking lot shook his hand, looked him in the eye, and deposited love in the depths of his soul. For several Sundays this interaction continued outside the church doors. Jerry told me that he even slowed his steps if the man had his back turned, waiting for the man to see him. Not long afterward, someone led Jerry to the Lord. Who was the greatest, the one who consistently showed love to a man who felt unloved or the person who actually led him to Christ?

A woman I know became pregnant. Her husband insisted she get an abortion. The day after the procedure, she was in the doctor's office for a follow-up visit. She stole the documents from her files, carried them from the office, and shredded them— hoping also to shred the memory from her mind. Now more than a decade later, hardly a day goes by that she doesn't wonder who the child might have become.

What if someone had been available to that woman—a friend to cry with, a person marching at the clinic who might have made her aware of the years of difficult memories to follow? Where were the "great" individuals that day?

Our Part

How did Jesus respond when asked who was the greatest in the kingdom? He summoned a child and said, "Whoever humbles himself like this child is the greatest in the kingdom of heaven" (Matthew 18:4).

"But," you might say, "all I have to give is a meager offering and encouraging words." If that's your feeling, this next story is for you.

Probably no one on the hillside listening to Jesus speak one day owned less than a boy who had just a few loaves and fishes. But after Jesus fed spiritual morsels to the throngs of people, He looked into their faces and also saw their hunger for natural food. So He asked the boy for what he held in his arms—two fish and five loaves of bread. Surely the boy must have thought, *What can you ever do with this little bit I have to give?* But he stretched out his hands and gave Jesus everything he had.

That meager gift was used by Jesus to feed 5,000 men, plus women and children, and even provided leftovers! God had an appointment with the boy that day to use what he had. No one else possessed exactly what the boy did at the time Jesus asked to use it. And the boy would never have known just how far his gift could go if he were not willing to give it away.

Who's the greatest? "Whoever humbles himself like this child is the greatest in the kingdom of heaven."

When my children were young, we used to read the book *Together*, by George Ella Lyon. The book says, "You salt the ice, and I'll crank the cream; let's put our heads together and dream the same dream." The Bible also discusses the importance of everyone doing his part: "Each one should use whatever gift he has received to serve others, faithfully administering God's grace in its various forms" (1 Peter 4:10).

God asks all of us to bring what we hold and lay it at His feet each day. Those He sees as the greatest are those who humbly offer what they have. God makes no class or marital distinctions. Each of us holds but one piece of the puzzle and but a single ingredient in the recipe. For this time and place, His hand is held out to each of us, asking for the baskets we hold. Who knows the baby our piece might help to save or the soul our part might reach? God knows. It's His puzzle, after all, and He sees the picture in its entirety, complete with your pieces and mine.

1. Take a look at what's in your basket today. What special gifts has God given to you?

2. How has He used those gifts in the past?

3. In what ways can you more freely share your gifts?

4. How might you encourage your children to develop their gifts?

"Well done, good and faithful servant! You have been faithful with a few things; I will put you in charge of many things. Come and share your master's happiness!" (Matthew 25:21).

35

A Foolproof Battle Plan

Struggles don't happen only in single-parent homes. Statistics say that only 20 percent of the challenges we face are because we're heading our homes alone.

Growing up in a Christian home enabled me to see and hear many individuals who trusted God through various struggles and over a long span of time. I watched their hair grow gray and their faces wrinkle as they told how God had remained faithful. Church dinners were consumed with everyone talking about recent battles that God had helped them through.

After I became the head of my home, I sometimes grew weary of the battles I faced—physical, financial, spiritual, and social. No sooner was I through one than I had to position myself for another. And that's what I did.

One of my favorite characters in the Bible is King Jehoshaphat. I've used his memorable battle in 2 Chronicles 20 as a model to find my own way to victory.

The Timeless Story

Jehoshaphat was a godly king in Judah. He faced war with the Moabites and Ammonites. When some men told Jehoshaphat about the vast size of the enemy armies, he began to form his battle plan.

• *He pulled together those he led.* "Alarmed, Jehoshaphat resolved to inquire of the Lord, and he proclaimed a fast for all Judah. The people of Judah came together to seek help from the Lord" (verses 3-4).

Since my children have gotten older, I find it beneficial to involve them in fighting our battles. I describe the challenge we face, and together we take it to God in prayer. This happens at bedtime following devotions, before meals, or before departing for school. I've also fasted while seeking wisdom for certain problems. Though I haven't yet asked the kids to fast, I have taught them about it from Isaiah 58. The important thing is that our family unit has rallied for the occasion. And my children will be able to take this skill into their later struggles as adults.

• *He modeled prayer for those he led.* Jehoshaphat stood before the assembly of Judah and prayed publicly, "If calamity comes upon us, whether the sword of judgment, or plague or famine, we will stand in your presence before this temple that bears your Name and will cry out to you in our distress, and you will hear us and save us. . . . For we have no power to face this vast army that is attacking us" (verses 9, 12).

Our kids need to see us put our faith in God. All the talk in the world doesn't hit home like looking straight to God when we face a formidable enemy. We let them know that we realize nothing is too big for God to handle.

I must admit that there have been times when my kids' faces looking to me for guidance were the only thing that kept this fact clear in my mind; otherwise, I would have conceded the battle in despair. But when I started praying again, we all found God faithful once more.

• *He acknowledged God's sufficiency.* "We do not know what to do, but our eyes are upon you," Jehoshaphat told God (verse 12).

It's easy to take the big I-can't-do-anything-about-this needs to God, but we sometimes neglect the smaller things. We need to show our children how to go to God for everything or we will botch things up.

• *He waited.* "All the men of Judah, with their wives and children and little ones, stood there before the Lord" (verse 13).

I've explained to my children my frustration with the waiting process. It's easy to trust God for the next step when you've just seen Him handle the last in some miraculous way. But what about the request you've had before Him for months? Does He really hear? Of course He does, and our kids need to have confidence in God's impeccable timing.

• *He listened.* "Then the Spirit of the Lord came upon Jahaziel. . . . He said, . . . 'This is what the Lord says to you: "Do not be afraid or discouraged because of this vast army. For the battle is not yours, but God's"'" (verses 14-15).

Others helped Jehoshaphat stay strong. He didn't try to fight the battle without support.

Everywhere we've lived, I have surrounded myself with strong people in the faith who loved me and my children. Then I could call them in time of trouble to pray. Often they offered wise words of advice or encouragement. Jahaziel did this for Jehoshaphat, and he listened to him.

• *He obeyed in God's timing.* "Tomorrow march down against them . . . you will find them at the end of the gorge. . . . Take up your positions; stand firm and see the deliverance the Lord will give you" (verses 16-17).

Jehoshaphat was careful not to get ahead of God. The people watched as he waited until the next day to take up his position. This is sometimes hard for one in leadership. Those following often want results to come more quickly. I've learned the hard way, however, that devastation comes from stepping ahead of God. I let my kids know it, too.

• *He placed his faith in God.* "'Do not be afraid; do not be discouraged. Go out to face them tomorrow, and the Lord will be with you.' Jehoshaphat bowed with his face to the ground, and all the people of Judah and Jerusalem fell down in worship before the Lord" (verses 17-18).

Never was there any question about who Jehoshaphat and his army served. He modeled and the others followed.

Do your neighborhood, school, and church know who your family serves? They need to see you come successfully through struggles you face by depending on the Lord.

I remember one spring when I was having difficulty with one of my children. I told a couple of other mothers about it at a soccer game. When summer was over and the new season began, both mothers asked about the situation. I felt a new confidence as I said the battle wasn't yet over but I knew everything would be okay. They saw my trust in God.

• *He built the faith of those he led.* "Early in the morning they left for the Desert of Tekoa. As they set out, Jehoshaphat stood and said, 'Listen to me. . . . Have faith in the Lord your God and you will be upheld; have faith in his prophets and you will be successful'" (verse 20).

I've had to be available a lot of nights when my children cried over something important to them. I listened to their words, sympathized, and then—without spiritualizing—we took it to God in prayer. This affirmed that Mom didn't know all the answers, but she knew where to go for them. What a valuable tool in the dark times of my children's lives!

• *He praised the Lord before the victory was complete.* "After consulting the people, Jehoshaphat appointed men to sing to the Lord and to praise him for the splendor of his holiness as they went out at the head of the army, saying, 'Give thanks to the Lord, for his love endures forever'" (verse 21).

Those around us need to see the meaning of faith in action—"being sure of what we hope for and certain of what we do not see" (Hebrews 11:1). The victory doesn't have to be complete to prove that God is able. Our actions prove that we know He is faithful to that which He has promised.

The Results

> As they began to sing and praise, the Lord set ambushes against the men of Ammon and Moab and Mount Seir who were invading Judah, and they were defeated. . . . [A]nd his men went to carry off their plunder, and they found among them a great amount of equipment and clothing and also articles of value—more than they could take away. There was so much plunder that it took three days to collect it. (verses 22, 25)

Was there any doubt?

I have come through financial and emotional battles that seemed unwinnable and have found my family better off and stronger than we ever were before. Only God can take something potentially devastating and use it for our good.

Of course, victory doesn't always come in the package we expect. It often looks different from what we hoped and does not seem like true victory until some point down the line. I recall a woman who was greatly disappointed when she didn't get the job she wanted. Only later, when she got the perfect job she *needed,* did she see how God had been working on her behalf.

How did Jehoshaphat and his men respond to the victory God gave them? "On the fourth day they assembled in the Valley of Beracah, where they praised the Lord. . . . Then, led by Jehoshaphat, all the men of Judah and Jerusalem returned joyfully to Jerusalem, for the Lord had given them cause to rejoice over their enemies. They entered Jerusalem and went to the temple of the Lord with harps and lutes and trumpets" (verses 26-28).

Too many times, we survive a battle and forget to thank God for the victory. But Jehoshaphat and his men made that their first priority upon returning home. I've often told my children that when they show gratitude for something I do for them, I just want to go out and do more. God is the same way.

What About the Battles to Come?

"The fear of God came upon all the kingdoms of the countries when they heard how the Lord had fought against the enemies of Israel. And the kingdom of Jehoshaphat was at peace, for his God had given him rest on every side" (verses 29-30).

What a wonderful privilege to serve a God who is alive and well! He knows everything you and I will ever face, and He holds the battle plan for our victories. Like Jehoshaphat's army, my "army" is learning that when hard times come, they need to pull together, pray, acknowledge God's sufficiency, wait, listen, obey, hold onto their faith, and praise God. When I'm long gone, this battle plan will remain effective. For our God "waits to give us rest on every side." What a wonderful truth to give to my children!

❧ ❧ ❧ ❧ ❧ ❧ ❧ ❧

1. List the battles you have already won.

2. List the battles you now face.

3. Describe ways you can:

> Pull together
>
> Pray
>
> Acknowledge God's sufficiency
>
> Wait
>
> Listen
>
> Obey
>
> Have faith
>
> Praise God

4. Commit these words to memory, and repeat them often: "The battle is not ours, but God's."

"If anyone does attack you, it will not be my doing; whoever attacks you will surrender to you" (Isaiah 54:15).

36

Leaving Your Children to God

In the Bible, I read about a mother whose example showed me how to trust God for my family's protection. This woman had two older children and an infant. Conditions in the area where they lived had deteriorated, and their safety was threatened because they believed in God. The mom did all she could do to protect her children, but when the life of her youngest son hung in the balance, she trusted his safety completely to the Lord.

Who was this mom? Jochebed. And her baby son? Moses.

Someone Who's Been There

I discovered who Jochebed was after my family and I had been in Colorado only two months. The time had come for my children to leave for a four-week visit with their dad. They had never been away from me that long, so I dreaded the date of their departure.

When that mid-July Saturday morning came, I tearfully put them on the airplane and then made my way home. I slept that afternoon— three times. By the time darkness fell, I was fully rested, and a long night lay ahead. It was then that I became afraid.

What if their dad doesn't watch them carefully? How will they endure four weeks void of all spiritual things? Who will they go see when they wake up scared at night?

A week of misery began. I hurt. I sulked. I worried. My preoccupation with the children's absence did not allow me to enjoy the silence and get the rest my body and spirit needed. The majesty of the Rocky Mountains outside my living room window became a blur through my tears as I counted the days till the children returned.

Facing My Fears

The next Sunday, I again started the day grieving for my children. I said my morning prayers and asked God to take care of them. And as I did, He quietly said to my spirit, "Jochebed."

Jochebed? Who is Jochebed? I thought.

Sitting in the pew that morning in church, I remembered the name. I looked in my Bible concordance but saw no such reference. The final song ended, and I was particularly aware of the lonely walk back to my car. At home that afternoon, I became determined to find this Jochebed in the Bible, if such a person existed.

And then I found her in Exodus 2:2-4:

> She became pregnant and gave birth to a son. When she saw that he was a fine child, she hid him for three months. But when she could hide him no longer, she got a papyrus basket for him and coated it with tar and pitch. Then she placed the child in it and put it among the reeds along the bank of the Nile. His sister stood at a distance to see what would happen to him.

God was saying to me, "Lynda, you've done all you can do for those children. Now put them into the basket, and leave the rest to Me." What did that mean?

Physical Basket

Jochebed and her husband were Hebrews, God's chosen people. They had lived undisturbed in Egypt for years. "Then a new king, who did not know about Joseph, came to power in Egypt" (Exodus 1:8). This new leader knew nothing of God's grace toward these people and felt threatened by their growth and prosperity. He issued an order to kill all the male infants belonging to the Hebrews, hoping to end the threat of future leaders emerging from the race. Jochebed's three-month-old son was among those who would surely die, and she put off the inevitable as long as she could. She wrapped Moses in the only protection she had, set him into the river, and released him to the unknown.

Jochebed must have worried for the physical safety of her little one. After all, the baby was only floating in a basket! What if it capsized? Or suppose a crocodile overtook him?

Like Jochebed, I discovered when my first child was just an infant that I could commit her physical safety to God whether I was near or far away. I claimed Scriptures like Psalm 91:11-12: "For he will command his angels concerning you to guard you in all your ways; they will lift you up in their hands, so that you will not strike your foot against a stone."

As I learned to count on God in this area, I was able to stop worrying.

Spiritual Basket

Moses was so young, and his world was so evil and uncertain. Even if he survived physically, could he possibly hold on to his spiritual heritage?

Every day, I send my kids out into neighborhoods and schools where so many things could happen to destroy their Christian witness. Worrying about those possibilities can remove the joy of the day.

When I become anxious about the power of that roaring lion, I say aloud another verse that puts the interloper into his place: "The eyes of the Lord range throughout the earth to strengthen those whose hearts are fully committed to him" (2 Chronicles 16:9).

And He has certainly shown himself strong in our behalf.

Emotional Basket

Jochebed released Moses into the unknown. She took the chance that her little boy would find someone else to call "Mother."

The key to Jochebed's faith and the fulfillment of God's plan was doing all she could do and then releasing the rest to God. I was privileged one afternoon to realize God was doing the same for my own son.

Clint was in kindergarten. He came home from school, and we snuggled on the couch, where I read to him from one of his favorite books. After a bit, he stopped my reading and looked at me, blinking back tears. "Mommy," he said, "what does it sound like when Jesus talks to you?"

I described as best I could the experience of close communication with God. Then he described something I shall never forget.

"One night before I was almost six years old, I was trying to go to sleep. Then I heard, 'Clint?'

"I looked up and didn't see anybody, but I knew it was Jesus 'cause He didn't talk to my ears, He talked here," Clint said as he patted his chest.

He continued his story.

"What?" Clint responded to the voice.

"I love you, Clint," he heard in reply.

God not only came to tell my son He loved him, but He even called him by name. Later Clint told me, "Mom, that wasn't the first time it happened to me. That was just the first time I knew who it was."

So what do I do when my children go to visit their dad and nothing is left to my control? How do I respond as I stand at the threshold of the teenage years and face all that could go wrong?

I place them in a basket. I put them in the bulrushes. I "Jochebed" them.

❦ ❦ ❦ ❦ ❦ ❦ ❦ ❦

1. In what areas do you need to "Jochebed" your kids? The physical? emotional? spiritual? something other?

2. What might that mean you need to do in practical terms?

"And all thy children shall be taught of the Lord; and great shall be the peace of thy children" (Isaiah 54:13, KJV).

37

Be Ready

When we single parents were expectant dads or moms, we packed suitcases ahead of time for that excited trip to the hospital. Our bags remained poised and ready in some accessible corner of the house until the appointed hour arrived.

When I read Matthew 25:1-13, I get that same excited feeling. It's a story that never loses its sense of wonder.

In that passage, Jesus compared the kingdom of heaven to 10 wedding attendants who were waiting for the bridegroom. Five of these young women were foolish. They took the oil lamps they would need if he came at night but forgot extra fuel. The other five were wise because they took oil in jars along with their lamps.

The bridegroom took a long time to arrive. Those who waited grew tired, impatient, and distracted. But at midnight, the call rang out: "Here's the bridegroom! Come out to meet him!" (verse 6).

All 10 attendants woke up. The foolish ones, now running out of oil, tried to borrow some from the wise ones. They, however, didn't have enough to share.

The foolish young women went out and bought what they needed. At last they were fully prepared. But it was too late. While they were gone, the bridegroom arrived. The five wise attendants went with him to the wedding banquet. The door was shut behind them.

When the foolish ones arrived, they tried to get into the house. But the bridegroom responded, "I tell you the truth, I don't know you" (verse 12).

The point of the story is that Jesus is the Bridegroom, and we, His followers, need to be ready for His return, which could come at any time.

Life Insurance

Five years after I became a single mom, I finished my doctorate. One of my fellow students was a bright woman who made many wrong choices. She lived her life with no restraints or values and no thought of what eternity would bring. She was graduating soon and had accepted a job with a prestigious university. We agreed to have dinner together one night before she left, and I met her at the restaurant.

We chatted through dinner. The woman told me about the insurance and retirement programs she had set up. She described with fondness the house she had purchased and listed what else she needed to do to get ready for the move.

The more she talked, the more obvious was her lack of faith in God. I cared for this woman and was afraid I might not have another opportunity to present the gospel message. Since we had developed a level of trust over the three years we had known each other, I began talking when her explanation ended.

"As you know, I'm a Christian," I said. "All people are different and going separate ways. Yet we all will face death. And after we die, we'll be judged and sent to heaven or to hell. While you're purchasing your life insurance, consider your insurance for eternity. What's the status of that?"

"I'm okay," she responded. "I chose my church because they aren't judgmental. I can do what I want without feeling guilty."

I continued with words I knew she would understand. "What would you think if you walked to that platform tomorrow to receive your diploma and found that all you had worked for was a fraud? No matter how hard you studied to get to that day, if you hadn't been following the right course, you wouldn't earn your diploma."

The woman and I parted with a hug in front of the restaurant that night, and I've never seen her since. But wherever she is, whatever she's doing, I hope she's now waiting for the Bridegroom with her lamp and her oil, anticipating His return.

How Is Our Wait?

Fact: Jesus is coming back some day, and maybe soon. Yet because His return seems so delayed, I fear we Christians are also tired, impatient, and distracted. We get busy with our 401(k) programs and life insurance and the hassles of making it day to day, and we forget to live for eternity. We buy for today as if there will be limitless tomorrows. And what about our kids? Are their bags packed? Have they trusted in Jesus as their Savior, and are they living as if they expect His return at any time?

Hebrews 11:8-10 describes us as strangers in a foreign country, just passing through on our way to a better place—a city whose builder is God. Are we living as though that's true and modeling it for our children?

Sometimes we have to ask ourselves, "What is my goal?" The answer should be to bring along as many souls as possible when we go to meet our Lord.

Living as Christians expectantly awaiting our Lord's return means we'll need a few key things. In your mind, open your suitcase and lay it across the bed so it can "hold" the following:

• We'll need a commitment that will keep us true for the long haul. The appointed day may be delayed uncomfortably long. But our determination will cause us to keep looking for His coming.

• We'll need to be free of distractions that could turn our thoughts and hearts away from Him. Let's get rid of those things that cause our faith to waver.

• We'll need to look ready. Others will watch us as we wait, and they should notice something different—something appealing—about our lives. We want them to want to come along when Jesus returns.

Jesus is coming soon. We need to live like it. We should position ourselves carefully to make an uncomplicated departure. We've got to keep our eyes open for that unknown day and hour. We must show our kids that we're being productive until He comes (see Luke 19:13). It puts a different perspective on everything—when we're packed and ready to go.

❧ ❧ ❧ ❧ ❧ ❧ ❧ ❧

1. Are you packed and ready to go?

2. What distractions, if any, keep you from living with the expectation of Jesus' imminent return?

3. What changes might you need to make in order to live more wisely?

"No one knows about that day or hour, not even the angels in heaven, nor the Son, but only the Father. Be on guard! Be alert!" (Mark 13:32-33).

38

I'll Follow You No Matter What

My father pastored a church in rural Indiana as my seven siblings and I were growing up. Our house was almost an hour's drive from the church, and four services a week kept us there often. I have many memories of that place and its people.

Jack Armond was in his late twenties, married, and the father of two small children. I watched Jack go to the altar to "pray through" on several occasions. Whenever the church held a series of revival services, Jack was there. Whenever emotions ran high, you could count on Jack to be one of those affected.

The problem was that as soon as the revival was over or the emotions died down, so did Jack's enthusiasm for the things of the Lord. His heart wasn't right. He went straight back to his life as an alcoholic and would regularly drink himself into oblivion. But this lifestyle eventually caught up with him.

Jack's heart wasn't right in another way, either. He had been born with a heart problem, and my dad went to the hospital to pray with him after he suffered a serious heart attack. For a while, it didn't look as if Jack would make it, but he did. And as soon as he was able, he came back to church—again.

One night, Jack stood before the congregation, his jet-black hair reflecting the light above. Tears dripped off his cheeks as he told us that the doctors gave him little hope for the future. "I'm ready to die for God," he said.

The words haunted me as a 13-year-old girl. I asked my dad about it on the way home, and I will never forget his response. "I believe Jack is, indeed, willing to die for God," Dad said, "but I don't think he's ready to live for Him."

Then one day, Jack was sitting in the car with his wife when he suffered another heart attack. His wife ran to the other side of the car and slid him over so she could drive to the hospital. "I just kept him leaning against me," she said. "I didn't want to admit that Jack was dead."

He left his wife and those tiny children to go on without him. We in the congregation also missed him—his smile, his tears, his tenderness. And though Jack died more than 30 years ago now, my dad's words have stayed with me: *He was willing to die for God, but he wasn't willing to live for Him.*

Not the Only One

Sometimes I see Jack crying and hear his words through other people. I listen to those who say in the bad times that they will serve God, but then they seem to forget their promise when things are okay. Others blame God for misfortunes: "How can He do this to me?" or "I don't think God likes me." They seem to feel God owes them something, and they're intent on collecting it. They carry grudges and hurl insults as they ask, "Why me?" Their lives show little of the commitment that comes with serving God.

Daniel 3 tells about three men who had an undying, unwavering commitment to God—Shadrach, Meshach, and Abednego. They were among the Hebrews taken into captivity by the Babylonian king Nebuchadnezzar when he conquered the kingdom of Judah.

The king made an idol of gold and announced that everyone in the kingdom must bow down and worship it. Those who refused would be thrown into a blazing furnace and burned alive.

The king's assistants told him, "But there are some Jews whom you have set over the affairs of the province of Babylon . . . who pay no attention to you. . . . They neither serve your gods nor worship the image of gold you have set up" (verse 12).

The king was angry. He summoned Shadrach, Meshach, and Abednego and said: "If you are ready to fall down and worship the image I made, very good. But if you do not worship it, you will be thrown immediately into a blazing furnace. Then what god will be able to rescue you from my hand?" (verse 15).

The response of the three young men was a testament to their faith in the one true God: "If we are thrown into the blazing furnace, the God we serve is able to save us from it, and he will rescue us from your hand, O king. But even if he does not, we want you to know, O king, that we will not serve your gods or worship the image of gold you have set up" (verses 17-18).

There's More

In the words of Paul Harvey, the well-known radio commentator, "And now for the rest of the story . . ."

The three Hebrews refused to bow their knees to a false god, and Nebuchadnezzar refused to be defied. So he cranked the furnace up seven times hotter than usual, then had them bound and thrown in. The heat was so great that it killed the soldiers who hurled them in.

But the expected did not happen. Soon the king was saying, "Weren't there three men that we tied up and threw into the fire? . . . Look! I see four men walking around in the fire, unbound and unharmed, and the fourth looks like a son of the gods" (verses 24-25).

It wasn't a son of the gods, however, but *the* Son of God who accompanied Shadrach, Meshach, and Abednego in their fiery furnace. And thanks to His intervention, they came out of the fire with no harm to their bodies, hair, or robes. Not even the smell of fire was upon them!

Settled Issues

We live in a society that holds shallow commitments. People are up one day and down the next. They stand for one thing on Tuesday and by Wednesday have changed their minds. A generation ago, men proudly died for their country. Because they were willing to do that, they also *lived* proudly for the principles upon which that country was founded. Today, because commitments tend not to run so deep, little seems worth living for. It takes courage to die for a belief or cause; even more courage is required to live for it. Dying for something takes one right choice; living for it requires hundreds of choices each day.

Nebuchadnezzar recognized what Shadrach, Meshach, and Abednego possessed: "They trusted in [God] and defied the king's command and were willing to give up their lives rather than serve or worship any god except their own God" (verse 28). That same commitment spilled over into their daily lives.

I woke up one morning recently to spend some time with God. My heart was heavy concerning some problems I needed Him to carry. But as I sat looking to Him for help, I said, "God, I give You my life today all over again. You're able to take care of these things. But even if You don't relieve this burden, I'll still serve You always. You owe me nothing, even though You give me everything."

That prayer freed me. It forced me off the fence and back onto a firm ground of commitment. It forged an unalterable, nonnegotiable principle upon which I could base all else, no matter how my circumstances changed. It made me define something I'm willing to die for—and to live for, no matter what.

✄ ✄ ✄ ✄ ✄ ✄ ✄ ✄

1. What things do you think are worth dying for?

2. What things *wouldn't* you die for?

3. What things do you live for each day?

4. How can you strengthen your commitment to the things that are worth living for?

"Yet I reserve seven thousand in Israel—all whose knees have not bowed down to Baal and all whose mouths have not kissed him" (1 Kings 19:18).

39

Dividing the Children

The story is old, but the truths it teaches are as real as if it had been written today—especially for single parents. It is found in 1 Kings 3:16-28.

Two women stood before King Solomon, each claiming to be the mother of a child. Solomon, known for his great wisdom, spoke slowly and confidently, "'Bring me a sword.' So they brought a sword for the king. He then gave an order: 'Cut the living child in two and give half to one and half to the other.'

"The woman whose son was alive was filled with compassion for her son and said to the king, 'Please, my lord, give her the living baby! Don't kill him!' . . .

"Then the king gave his ruling: 'Give the living baby to the first woman. Do not kill him; she is his mother.'

"When all Israel heard the verdict the king had given, they held the king in awe, because they saw that he had wisdom from God to administer justice."

Splitting the Time

The breakup of a family nearly always signals turmoil. The parties who once declared their love for each other now would like to have no further contact.

But when children are involved, that can never be. Too often, the children become objects of manipulation, as one parent tries to gain an edge on the other.

Even if you've experienced extreme deceit and treachery at the hands of a former partner and getting revenge seems reasonable, don't do it. Don't put your kids in the position of having to divide their love and loyalties between their two parents.

That other person will always be the parent of your children, and your kids will always need both of you. Researcher Claudia Jewett, in studying grief, says the length of time it takes children to heal depends on the number of life changes they experience and how much strife continues between the parents.

Now is the time to become as wise as Solomon concerning your children who are being "cut in two." Put your hurts behind you, and do what's best for your kids. Save your children before it's too late.

• *Don't let them blame themselves.* Children usually feel the family breakup is their fault. Both parents should explain that while they don't love each other anymore, their love for the children goes on. Kids need to understand they're not responsible for the failure of the parents' relationship. At the same time, help your children release unrealistic expectations that you and your former mate will get back together, especially if one of you has married someone else.

• *Share their enthusiasm.* Strive hard to share your kids' enthusiasm over things they do while with the other parent. Talk openly about the zoo they're going to on Saturday or the picture they drew two weeks ago at Dad's. Too many times, children feel like a traitor while at the other parent's house. Reassure them they are not. Allow them to talk openly about their experiences and feelings, and respond with positive comments and facial gestures.

• *Don't ask questions.* Refrain from pumping your kids for information about the other parent. If they relate a conflict or difficulty they've experienced, remain neutral. If necessary, talk privately with your former mate.

• *Remain available.* Your children are going to need to talk. Spend time alone together in a neutral place while biking, hiking, or walking. Listen carefully, and answer their questions.

• *Stay flexible.* Make concrete arrangements for visitation, and change them as rarely as possible. When adjustments are necessary, however, cooperate in every way possible. On holidays, set up an alternating schedule, or choose to celebrate on different days altogether. Most of all, talk with your children's other parent.

• *Resist negative talk.* In the early years, it was especially hard for me to hear my children declare their undying love for their father over the phone. I somehow thought it was my duty to inform them of what he had done wrong. But someone gave me wise counsel: "Don't say anything negative about their father. They'll know what they need to know when the time is right." The no-negative-talk rule also applies when you're dialoging with another adult within the hearing range of your kids. Children often take on characteristics of both parents and will blame themselves when they hear critical words from someone they love. Instead, they need to see you model love, respect, and the forgiveness of Christ.

• *Pray together regularly for your children's other parent.* When my older daughter, Ashley, was five, my divorce became final, and we moved to another state. One day she came home from a stay with her dad. She indicated with tears in her eyes that she wanted to talk with me after her brother and sister went to bed.

Later Ashley came to the family room couch and climbed on my lap. "Mommy," she said, "Daddy got really mad at me this weekend, and he said he wouldn't. He came in to say good night to me, and I told him I knew exactly what he needed. Before I told him, I made him promise not to get mad.

"Then I told him he needed to ask Jesus to come and live in his heart so he would be happy. But Daddy got really mad and yelled at me. It scared me, Mommy."

I held her close as we both cried. Then I said this prayer:

"Lord, if Ashley and I went into the backyard, dug a hole in the earth, dropped in a seed, and covered it, we wouldn't see it anymore. But with your rain and sunshine to provide refreshment and nourishment, that seed would take root. Over a period of time, as the plant sprouted, we could see it slowly break through the soil and begin to grow into a strong and living plant. All that would begin with just one seed.

"Your Word says, 'I have planted, Apollos watered; but God gave the increase' (1 Corinthians 3:6). You need for us to plant the seeds of the love of Jesus Christ in all those around us. Then it's up to You to make them grow.

"This weekend, Ashley planted a seed in her daddy. When she did, it appeared to be lost. But we believe that with Your nourishment, that seed can come forth as new life for Daddy. So as we go about our play and remain a testimony, we leave it up to You to provide what's necessary for that seed to grow. Thank You, Lord. Amen."

Praying together for someone makes it totally impossible to hold on to bad feelings. Do it when you're alone as well. God longs to soften your heart and to heal the hurts you feel.

Today's sacrifices for your children will pay big dividends later on. Don't divide their loyalties no matter how much pain you've suffered. Some things are just worth letting go of. The desire for revenge, especially through your kids, is most certainly one of them.

❧ ❧ ❧ ❧ ❧ ❧ ❧ ❧

1. What difficulties do you still encounter in your children's visitation with the other parent?

2. How can you keep from "cutting the children in two" in the following areas?

Don't let them blame themselves.

Share their enthusiasm.

Don't ask questions.

Remain available.

Stay flexible.

Resist negative talk.

Pray together.

"Do not forsake wisdom, and she will protect you; love her, and she will watch over you" (Proverbs 4:6).

40

Seasons of Change

It was late fall, the nine-year anniversary of my becoming a single mom and subsequently surrendering to Christ. The afternoon sun spotlighted the yellow edges of the aspen leaves in the yard. Hues of golds, yellows, browns, and deep greens lined the horizon as far as the eye could see. Goldenrods, cattails, and brown thistles swayed proudly in the field behind our home as a flock of Canada geese honked purposefully overhead. The crisp wind filtered through the opening of the window where I sat pondering what else needed to be accomplished that day. A potpourri of autumn smells rushed into the kitchen. Summer flowers displayed last-minute blossoms before the first frost. Change was in the air.

Inside, the house was shrouded in silence. But soon it became a hub of activity as the children burst through the doors from school, backpacks in hand. Their search for something to fill their empty tummies was disrupted only by their unison explanations of the day's activities—spelling test results; paint spilled during art; a new friend found during recess.

Clint, in third grade, paused for a hug, then disappeared into his room. Soon he was back in the kitchen with clothes changed, baseball mitt tucked firmly under his arm, and his cap perched backward on his head. He leaned against his bat and devoured a peanut butter sandwich. After downing a tall glass of milk, he moved toward the door, punching his fist into the palm of his glove.

Courtney, in fifth grade, talked nonstop about her school day, then announced she was going to feed Thumper. In a few minutes, she called to me through the open window to hand her a carrot for the plump, white rabbit, pink eyes wide with anticipation.

Ashley, in seventh grade, walked slowly through the door, aimlessly reading the last pages of a book. Conversation was sparing until the book was complete; then she gave chapter-by-chapter details. She asked me to remember soccer practice later as she picked up the phone and dialed one of her friends with whom she had just spent the day. "Hi. Whatcha doing?" she said.

This was an ordinary day in what is often described as a "broken home." The normalcy reflects God's bountiful riches. Not every day of the previous nine years had been that way, however: Many brought turbulent storms. I had fought hard to hold on to what I thought would restore us to wholeness, and I was reluctant to let go of those things I still controlled. Even today we continue to battle hardships, and often that which we have counted on the most has been the first to go.

But on that fall day, as the brilliance of autumn splashed over the lives of my family, I paused to enjoy its splendor. I realized other cold winters would follow, for life is a process, and change is inevitable.

As I think of the changes, I remember the trips my children and I have taken to see maple syrup made. The more frequent and extreme the temperature changes in an area, the better the quality of the sap. The sap is produced throughout the cold of the winter months. Then springtime comes to the maple trees, which seem dead and lifeless. But the sap that was made through cold times begins to flow out into the buckets and vats. It takes 40 gallons of sap to make one gallon of syrup. But once you taste the golden syrup on a stack of pancakes, you know that both the process and extremes in temperature have been worth it.

In the same way, while I know more winters are ahead, I have the eternal assurance of a coming springtime that brings new hope and life and joy.

Certain things remain a mystery to me, but others I know for sure. I know I have no desire to return to the things I held so closely and fought so hard to keep. I know God has promised to take care of my children and me no matter what comes. And I know everything in our lives will keep on changing except for that one eternal, all-sufficient, unchangeable hand onto which I hold. I just know!

While the seasons around us are always changing, the Scriptures are as enduring as they've always been. I can draw strength and comfort in knowing that what He promises today will always be the same.

Still, you may say . . .

❦ ❦ ❦ ❦ ❦ ❦ ❦ ❦

1. "But you don't know all the changes we've gone through. When will we ever feel stable again?"

Read 2 Corinthians 4:16-18. Then list as many things as you can think of that have changed for you and your family since being on your own. (e.g., "I have no one to help me with these countless tasks.")

Changes   *Results*

Beside each of those changes, write the results that have occurred (e.g., "I have found only God is dependable, consistent, and true. My relationship with Him has grown as a result of that fact.")

2. "But you don't know all I lost and all the plans that were destroyed!"

Read Matthew 6:19-21. Then list your priorities—the things that have become more important to you than anything else since becoming a single parent.

How are these different from before?

3. "Can I really count on anything not changing or letting me down?"

Read and memorize James 1:17: "Every good and perfect gift is from above, coming down from the Father of the heavenly lights, who does not change like shifting shadows."

Also memorize Psalm 105:8: "He remembers his covenant forever, the word he commanded, for a thousand generations."

That means our children too!

4. "But I keep remembering how it used to be and all the things my children have missed."

Read 2 Corinthians 5:17 and Philippians 3:12. Then list all the things from the past that you would like to let go.

Finally, pray this prayer:

"Father, You instruct me in Your Word to forget what is behind and to strain toward what is ahead. I can't do this without You. I need You to help me forget _____, _____, and _____. Keep my eyes from looking behind. Instead, help me look forward to what You have that's better for my family and me. And thank You, God, because in the face of everything that has changed, Your Word and Your faithfulness to me will never change. Amen."

"Jesus Christ is the same yesterday and today and forever" (Hebrews 13:8).

41

Stay in Touch

One of the special things about being a mom is the affectionate touches I get. My family and I have found the most creative ways to cram multiple bodies together on the couch at the end of a long day. In church, my shoulders have supported heads on both sides through many Sunday morning sermons.

I became intrigued with touching, however, long before I was a mom.

One morning in May when I was married, my husband had left for work, and I was getting ready to do the same. We lived next door to my husband's mom and dad and helped them with their 40 horses. Suddenly I heard my father-in-law calling for help. I looked out the back window and saw him standing with a horse in the field.

I called work to say I'd be late, changed my clothes in a moment, and bolted out the door. My father-in-law was a retired veterinarian, and I immediately knew he was helping the mare get through a complicated birth. After we had worked for a while, he discovered she was having twins.

I didn't know till later what a rare occurrence that was, but in the brilliance of the glistening dew of that Indiana field that morning, I helped bring forth new lives. Two chestnut foals lay on the ground, unsteadily looking around as if to say, *Are we there yet?*

That's when the touching began. The mother nudged, poked,

stroked, and licked at her babies all over their wet bodies. My father-in-law later told me that this licking was essential for adequate organic and behavioral development of the babies. If they weren't licked, they wouldn't survive.

For some reason, before long the mare stopped licking one of the babies—the one that appeared stronger at first. Nothing we could do made her regain her interest, and the next day the foal died.

The Right Touch

For people as well, touching has always served an important function. Skin is the most sensitive of our organs and is our protector and first medium of communication. Touching is referred to in all kinds of contexts: We speak of "rubbing people the wrong way" and "stroking" them the right way. We know "abrasive" and "prickly" personalities, but we like to be around those with "soft touches." Some are "thick-skinned," while others are "thin-skinned" and must be "handled" with care. I get "touchy" now and then, but that's better than being "out of touch" or "losing my grip."

Touching also serves important functions in the Bible. One example is found in Mark 5:21-34.

Jesus had just crossed the Sea of Galilee, and a large crowd came to see Him, including a woman who had been hemorrhaging for 12 years. She had gone everywhere and spent all her money trying to get help. But she knew one touch from Jesus would make her okay. So as He walked by, she touched His cloak.

That touch immediately stopped the bleeding in the woman, and it also stopped Jesus dead in His tracks. He felt power go out of Him, and He asked, "Who touched my clothes?"

The woman acknowledged her contact with Him, and Jesus said, "Daughter, your faith has healed you. Go in peace and be freed from your suffering."

This supernatural power in His touch was nothing new to Jesus. No matter where He traveled, He touched lives by touching bodies. "And wherever he went—into villages, towns or countryside—they placed the sick in the marketplaces. They begged him to let them touch even the edge of his cloak, and all who touched him were healed" (Mark 6:56).

Sometimes the touching practices of Jesus were unorthodox, but those who benefited didn't care. "They came to Bethsaida, and some people brought a blind man and begged Jesus to touch him. He took the blind man by the hand and led him outside the village. When he had spit on the man's eyes and put his hands on him . . . " (Mark 8:22-23).

Children were particularly important to Jesus. Much the same way children like to touch everything in sight, they must have touched Jesus—both physically and in His heart: "People were bringing little children to Jesus to have him touch them. . . . And he took the children in his arms, put his hands on them and blessed them" (Mark 10:13-16).

Touching. It was the connection between what Jesus had and what the people needed.

The Lasting Touch

Jesus isn't physically with us anymore. Yet He left His touch behind. When I get the most tired and discouraged, I picture myself climbing up into His lap and having Him play with my hair. The cares of the day seem to melt away, and He makes me strong and ready to go again.

As important as touch is to me, I often forget to share it with my kids when I come home from a full-time job. I'm tired and intent on making it through the dinner and homework hours.

Then three kids meet me at the door, bombarding me with messages and instructions about what needs to be done. Overwhelmed, I often want to retire to the quietness of my room.

One day at the beginning of the school year, Courtney came home from her third-grade class and handed me a crumpled lunch bag as I prepared dinner. I opened it to some strange contents and a scrap of paper bearing this message written by her teacher:

In this bag you will find:
Rubber bands to remind you of hugging and those times
when you want to give a hug or when you just want
to receive one.
Tissue to remind you to dry someone's tears away.
Toothpick to pick out all the good qualities of
someone.
Candy kisses to remind you that people need a treat
once in a while.
Eraser to remind you that everyone makes mistakes
and that's okay.

I read the reminder through my tears and looked up at a young girl who was already on the run through the house. I lay down the spoon I held and picked up a little boy with eyes full of adventure. I ruffled Courtney's hair and tickled her, realizing again how tall she was going to be. I winked at Ashley and gave her a quick hug as she did her usual thing on the phone. I had been reminded one more time of the most special way to stay in touch with my kids.

❦ ❦ ❦ ❦ ❦ ❦ ❦ ❦

1. Do you need to receive a special touch today? Picture yourself crawling up into the lap of Jesus as the children did in the Bible. Imagine Him stroking your hair or whatever is comforting to you. Then talk to Him. He's listening.

2. Do you need to *give* a special touch today? What specific things can you do within the bounds of propriety? Select at least five people who can benefit from your special touch.

> Your children?

> A neighbor?

> A co-worker?

"People were bringing little children to Jesus to have him touch them. . . . And he took the children in his arms, put his hands on them and blessed them" (Mark 10:13, 16).

42

My Garden,
My Church

When my children were five, three, and one, we went from a familiar home in the suburbs to a small apartment in a new city with new
surroundings and new people. I worked as a teaching assistant at a
university and carried 18 hours in a doctoral program.

Meanwhile, the divorce was not yet final, and my dad was dying of an
incurable disease. Although the children maintained an alternating-week-
end visitation with their father, we had no family nearby.

I soon learned more about God's leading, however, as He began to
use the church of which we became a part to help put our lives
together again. Little by little, people addressed the many issues my
family and I faced every day.

A Song of Songs passage eloquently describes the role the church
played during that vulnerable time in our lives. I'm aware that many
Bible scholars see that book simply as Solomon's poem about roman-
tic love. It has also spoken to me and others, however, as a metaphor of
God's love for His people.

> You are a garden locked up, my sister, my bride;
>   you are a spring enclosed, a sealed fountain.
> Your plants are an orchard of pomegranates
>   with choice fruits,
>   with henna and nard,

> nard and saffron,
> calamus and cinnamon,
> with every kind of incense tree,
> with myrrh and aloes
> and all the finest spices.
> You are a garden fountain,
> a well of flowing water
> streaming down from Lebanon.
> (Song of Songs 4:12-15)

At the church we attended, I found a group of lovely people who hadn't a clue about what it means to be a single parent—the schedule, the physical demands, the emotional and financial load. They were busy with many wonderful ministries to areas outside the church. Meanwhile, my personal pain was much closer to me than the foreign missions they supported. But because I had nowhere else to turn for support, I became involved in the church and made our needs known.

We needed spiritual food. Solomon described "an orchard of pomegranates with choice fruits." In the Old Testament, when the people of Israel were wandering in the wilderness, they sighed for the abandoned comforts of Egypt, including the cooling pomegranates. Some legends say the Tree of Life in the Garden of Eden was a pomegranate. But to me, the "orchard of pomegranates" became the knowledge I needed about the character of Christ and where He fit into the lives of my children and me.

I heard ministers and Sunday school teachers deliver powerful sermons and stirring testimonies that moved me beyond words. Musicians proclaimed the truth of the gospel in melody, influencing me to lean further on the Lord on my own. From that spiritual food, I found nourishment and strength not only to survive, but also to grow.

We needed new color and fresh scents in our lives. My family had lost a great deal, and much remained that was hard and disheartening. The garden described by Solomon was also endowed "with henna and nard and saffron."

Henna was a highly scented plant used to color hair, fingernails, and the soles of the feet. Saffron, which was sprinkled in the streets when the emperor Nero made his entry into Rome, was worth more than its weight in gold. I found myself looking for ways to color *our* lives. Most valuable were the individuals who became our friends—embracing, listening, loving, and calling us to accountability.

I remember an anonymous person whose envelopes of money kept coming during a time when I was out of work. There was the man who became a mentor to my son and the couple who offered to replace the headlight in my car. These "colors" spilled onto the canvas of my children's lives as they, too, found individuals who took time to know each of them. Such people became like saffron, worth more than their weight in gold.

Nard was obtained from a rare Himalayan plant. It was extremely valuable and was stored in alabaster boxes. Mary broke the seal on such a box and poured a pint of nard over Jesus just days before He died. Such an act was the highest form of honor a commoner could bestow on royalty. Onlookers chided Mary for the gross "waste." But she unreservedly poured out all she had onto her Master.

Scripture says, "And the house was filled with the fragrance of the perfume" (John 12:3). Jesus said, "Whatever you did for one of the least of these brothers of mine, you did for me" (Matthew 25:40). Think of what our churches would be like if each of us poured love and grace without reservation on those around us. Imagine the fragrance in our churches and the needs that would be met!

We needed zest—something to which we could look forward. Solomon wrote of "calamus and cinnamon," which are used to season food. The church has the ability to season the lives of all its members.

One Fourth of July when my children were gone, a young couple, Mark and Marcy, asked me to their cookout. An otherwise lonely day was spent with friends who made me feel special. My family and I looked forward to the invitations and activities at the church, where we could fit in and become a part. It truly added zest to our existence. Some of our dearest relationships will always be with those who took time to spice up our lives.

Finally, *we needed healing* "with every kind of incense tree, with myrrh and aloes." All single parents, whether they're never married, divorced, or widowed, come wounded to the sanctuary door. They're in desperate need of restoration. In the garden described by Solomon, the myrrh was used as an antiseptic and an astringent to deaden pain and relieve soreness. Even today, there's nothing like aloe to heal burns, large or small. I found myrrh and aloe in those who listened and prayed and cared about our family's special needs. They helped me channel my efforts and pick up the pieces from the shattered world so overwhelming to me then.

Fellow Christians, let's stand up! Let's look around and see the important role we can play in the lives of those who sit around us in our churches.

> Awake, north wind,
>> and come, south wind!
> Blow on my garden,
>> that its fragrance may spread abroad.
> Let my lover come into his garden
>> and taste its choice fruits.
> (Song of Songs 4:16)

When we in our churches open our eyes to the rich garden we are, the "fragrance" spreads far and wide. May we realize that in the church lies the provision for every man, woman, boy, and girl. May we remember why God established the church in the first place—not for the opulent walls that human hands have constructed but for supplying the needs of the people inside.

Song of Songs 5:1 continues to talk about the garden. We've already established the church's potential to minister to every member. But the action verbs in this verse hand some responsibility back to us as they describe one individual's entry into that garden.

꙰ ꙰ ꙰ ꙰ ꙰ ꙰ ꙰ ꙰

1. "*I have come* into my garden, my sister, my bride; *I have gathered* my myrrh with my spice."

What have you done to find a church that meets the needs of your family? The church can better help when you begin to help yourself.

On a piece of paper, list your needs. What can you do for yourself? And what exactly can the church do to help?

2. "*I have eaten* my honeycomb and my honey; *I have drunk* my wine and my milk."

You're responsible for your own spiritual development. What can you do to enhance your growth in the Lord?

3. Finally, "*Eat, O friends, and drink;* drink your fill, O lovers."

Remember, you're part of the church. You won't always be the "taker," the recipient of others' ministry. Part of your own healing will come in your outreach to others.

How can you extend a helping hand to three other people in their specific needs? How can you get them to the garden to also eat and drink?

Food? Color? Spice? Healing? What do you hold in your "alabaster box" to offer to the fragrance of the church? Remember, yours is like no one else's.

"Let my lover come into his garden and taste its choice fruits" (Song of Songs 4:16).

43

Make Me Your Vessel

When I was a child, I spent many sunny afternoons playing at the creek below our house. I can still feel the chill of the bubbling water around my feet. I would pull gray clay from beneath layers of rock, squeeze its moisture through my fingers, and roll the clay between my palms. Beads of charcoal-colored water sometimes ran down my arm and dripped from my elbow. Once I had gathered my trove of clay clumps, I would deposit them on a flat rock nearby, find a comfortable position where I could sit, and begin to make dishes for my playhouse.

I would start by removing the stones from the clumps of clay. It would never do to create my fine china with rocks that would mar the surface. So I pounded, rolled, squeezed, and even stomped on this clay to remove its impurities. In the process, the clay often dried out, so I would have to remoisten it with more creek water.

Finally, the prepared clay would be ready for molding. I would carefully decide how many plates and cups I needed and start working. I would pound a base with my fist, then wind the sides in a circular motion until they reached the right height. Next, I would smooth out the holes, dents, and bubbles with more moist pressure and line up the dishes on another rock to dry in the sun. The following day, I would check them. Sometimes a piece had cracked around an undetected stone or weak wall, and it had to be redone. But usually my plates and cups were dry and ready to be painted. Only after the painting was my work complete.

Different Waters

As I got bigger, so did life's challenges. My playhouse became a real house. Instead of wading in the cool, lazy creek, I found myself often struggling in deep waters. And rather than being the potter creating her own designs, I became the clay—pounded, rolled, squeezed, and stepped on.

When my husband left me, I experienced the greatest pain I had ever known. Not only did the hard knocks and squeezes hurt, but the waiting and the inability to do anything about the circumstances caused frustration. Nothing of consequence had disrupted my tranquil life before, and when people had talked to me about their troubles, I hadn't been able to relate to them. That was going to change.

When I surrendered my life to God upon becoming a single parent, I expected Him to take away all my pain. He didn't, and it wasn't until later that I realized how much God had to change me to make me into a usable vessel. (Actually, I'm still learning about that.)

During this time of discomfort, I continually sought the Lord's guidance in His Word. While reading in the book of Jeremiah, I came across the following passage:

> This is the word that came to Jeremiah from the Lord: "Go down to the potter's house, and there I will give you my message." So I went down to the potter's house, and I saw him working at the wheel. But the pot he was shaping from the clay was marred in his hands; so the potter formed it into another pot, shaping it as seemed best to him.
>
> Then the word of the Lord came to me: "O house of Israel, can I not do with you as this potter does?" declares

the Lord. "Like clay in the hand of the potter, so are you in my hand, O house of Israel." (18:1-6)

My childhood experience as an amateur potter came flooding back as I read those verses. I was amazed to learn that the word *Jeremiah* actually means "Jehovah throws." I went to the library and found books on pottery that gave me a deeper understanding of what this passage meant.

The Process

To a potter, "throwing" actually means to "make" or "create." The potter's business is to create things. He begins with worthless, decomposed granite that's filled with impurities and throws it onto his wheel. That's why God chose the potter's house to communicate His message to Jeremiah. God has something important to say to us in the dirty, undesirable workplaces of our lives.

The "wheel" mentioned in Jeremiah 18:3 is where the potter works on his raw materials. If the piece of clay becomes spoiled, he stops the wheel and smashes it with his fist. The potter is not only good at creating, but also at re-creating.

Why is the potter so picky? Because each piece is unique and bears the potter's trademark—his own fingerprints. If a dent or air bubble is allowed to remain, the piece will burst when heated in the kiln. But when a defect is found, the potter doesn't throw away the lump of clay and start over with a new piece. Rather, he throws the defective piece back on the wheel, puts his hands firmly around it, and begins his work anew. He's adept at doing several things to remake the vessel:

• *Wedging.* The potter kneads the clay, much like a baker working dough. This activity removes all traces of air and foreign matter and is often done by cutting clay slabs in half and pounding them. The clay then becomes soft, pliable, and easy to work with. Nothing else can be done until this process is complete.

• *Centering.* After the clay is ready to be worked, the potter throws it down hard in the dead center of the wheel. Both hands pull the clay to keep it there.

• *Pressuring.* The potter applies this squeezing maneuver in order to create the desired shape. When the clay dries out as he's working, he remoistens it by dipping his fingers in a nearby bowl of water before continuing.

Now the pot is ready to go into the furnace. Here, it receives a bisque—or first firing—and then it's decorated. Finally it's glazed. This glazing seals, hardens, and waterproofs the pot. How valuable the pot becomes depends on how high the furnace is turned. Earthenware, the least valuable, is made below temperatures of 2,000 degrees. Stoneware is a better quality and is fired at temperatures above 2,300 degrees. Finally, porcelain is created when the pot is subjected to the highest temperatures of all—above 2,670 degrees.

A Backward Glance

Once, as I was going through a tough waiting period and was seemingly getting nowhere with my plans, I took my children to an out-of-town play. As we drove home, they fell asleep, and I found myself talking to God in the silence of the car. "Why is it You seem to leave us so alone with no direction during times of pain?" I cried out.

Suddenly, He brought to my mind some areas that had changed during that past year—not the circumstances themselves but the ways I was dealing with them. I recalled emotional and spiritual challenges that had left me powerless in the past but were now causing me less concern. I was standing stronger, waiting better, and growing more sure of myself in the Lord each day.

That's when I realized that at times when I thought nothing was happening, something *was* happening. As long as I stayed "moistened" and pliable by the Word of God, He was able to squeeze out the impurities in my life and mold me more into His image.

One recent weekend, I was flying home from a conference where I had just spoken. The faces and tears of those I had met were still fresh in my mind. I thought of the big problems each of them had brought.

Could I have addressed that group of hurting people a few years before in my pre-squeezing, pre-punching, pre-remolding days? No. But God loved me enough to strengthen me for my own trials and to enable me to help others during theirs. Though I'm still far from finished, God had used the circumstances in my life to wedge, center, and pressure me into a better person.

As the plane began its descent, I prayed quietly for the people I had met and for God's continued work in me. And then I smiled as I remembered the words to a song that just about said it all:

> Have Thine own way, Lord, have Thine own way.
> Thou art the potter, I am the clay.
> Mold me and make me after thy will,
> While I am waiting, yielded and still.

❧ ❧ ❧ ❧ ❧ ❧ ❧ ❧

1. Before God could make great use of Moses, Jonah, or David, He first placed them on the potter's wheel. Where was that potter's wheel for each of them? (See Exodus 3, Jonah 1, and 1 Samuel 16 respectively.)

2. We can resist coming to the potter's wheel for the wedging, centering, and pressuring. But our resistance only contributes to our misery. How have you resisted His molding process in the past?

3. In your devotions over the next week, make this your heartfelt prayer to God: "Make me Your vessel."

"Yet, O Lord, you are our Father. We are the clay, you are the potter; we are all the work of your hand" (Isaiah 64:8).

44

Prioritize

It was a Thursday night. As I was tying together loose ends before flying to a conference the next day, I returned a phone call and discovered that a friend, Michael, had suddenly died. The man I talked to told how Michael had called him after they had taken a trip together. "I went for some routine tests," Michael had said. "The doctors found cancer everywhere. They didn't give me much time."

Thirty days later, Michael was dead.

The next morning I took my seat on the plane. I was still reliving memories of Michael and his wife and daughter. They had lived in an apartment beside my children and me after my divorce. Michael had brought his family to Ohio to help found a large Christian school, and then he became headmaster. Michael was so young and full of life. What would become of his plans? Of his daughter, who was only 14? And then I wondered, *What were those last 30 days like when life came to a standstill for Michael?*

The man on the phone had told me Michael would stare at everyone who came to see him in the hospital during that last month. "No one had a clue," Michael had said. "No one understood. I had nothing in common with anyone. Everyone had their own things to deal with."

My mind was pulled back to the present as the flight attendant gave take-off instructions. "In case of emergency, leave all your personal belongings behind," she cautioned.

Leave It!

"Leave your personal belongings behind." The words still echoed as the plane made its ascent. I opened my Bible and began reading in Matthew 24. I needed to hear a word from God.

My mind imagined what the setting of that passage might have been like. The sun was reflecting off the white marble of Herod's temple. My Bible commentary says this structure was one of the great wonders of ancient times. It stood 15 stories tall, and some of its stones were 94 feet long, 10 feet high, and 13 feet wide.

"Take a look at those awesome marble pillars!" the disciples must have said as they tilted back their heads and opened their eyes wide in wonder.

At the pinnacle of their enthusiasm, Jesus spoke. "'Do you see all these things?' he asked. 'I tell you the truth, not one stone here will be left on another; every one will be thrown down'" (Matthew 24:2).

"What? When? How will we know this is about to happen?" The disciples wanted to know more.

Jesus told them that many would try to deceive them, and many would succumb. Wars would take place. The believers would be handed over to be persecuted and even die. "But he who stands firm to the end will be saved" (Matthew 24:13).

"But won't there be time to grab a few things before we go?" the disciples probably asked. "It's not like we're strangers to you, Jesus."

He replied, "Let no one on the roof of his house go down to take anything out of the house. Let no one in the field go back to get his cloak" (Matthew 24:17).

Only the Essentials

Jesus' words to the disciples still spoke to me that day on the plane. His message was similar to the flight attendant's: "In case of emergency, leave your personal belongings behind." I also read Psalm 90:12, which says: "Teach us to number our days aright, that we may gain a heart of wisdom."

But how do we number our days? How do we make the most of our busy time on this earth and attend only to things that truly matter?

I remembered an incident during the latter days of my mother-in-law's life when I went to visit her in a nursing home on Christmas Day. My children were with their father, and it seemed sad that their grandmother lay so alone inside the prison her stroke had created. I talked and read her the Christmas story from Luke 2. I prayed with her and said good-bye—all to empty eyes and trembling lips. On my way out, I stopped briefly to tell a story and sing a song to other elderly people in the cafeteria.

When I returned to my car, the smells and oppression from where I had just been overwhelmed me. I put my head against the steering wheel and cried, "Is this all there is to look forward to?"

Later that evening, I found these words in Scripture: "Since my youth, O God, you have taught me, and to this day I declare your marvelous deeds. Even when I am old and gray, do not forsake me, O God, till I declare your power to the next generation, your might to all who are to come" (Psalm 71:17-18).

That passage plus my visit to the nursing home drove home the point that we need, indeed, to number our days and prioritize our efforts. This is true for a child who has a long life ahead, a man like Michael who is in the prime of life but has no guarantee about tomorrow, and a woman who's getting on in years. We all need to make the most of every hour and every day.

God must rejoice with His people when they understand this message *before* an emergency occurs. He must be pleased when He sees them not getting hung up with collecting material things or devoting their lives to vocational goals that will all have to be left behind.

As single parents, most of us are in the perfect place to avoid such pitfalls. We don't have the luxury of amassing great riches or names for ourselves. Instead, we stay busy raising our children—the ones who matter most—and doing the work He has called us to do.

One day recently, I was 24 hours away from a deadline at work. I went to a restaurant for a quick lunch. During the 20 minutes I was there, I led my waiter to Christ. Suddenly the computer screen on my desk wasn't as important; my deadline wasn't so daunting. They would be left behind if I died that night. But that waiter wouldn't. When his time came, he would join me in heaven.

God is teaching me to number my days. He's showing me how to concentrate my efforts on the things that will never be left behind. He's training me to declare His power to the next generation—no matter how much time I have left.

Thank You, God, for showing me that *before* the emergency comes.

✖ ✖ ✖ ✖ ✖ ✖ ✖ ✖

1. Imagine you've been given 30 days to live. List everything you would do the same as you are now.

2. List everything you would do differently.

3. What are you spending your time on that would need to be left behind in the event of an emergency?

4. What can you leave behind *before* an emergency occurs?

5. What important take-with-you things can you use to replace the nonessential?

"Occupy till I come" (Luke 19:13, KJV).

45

Be Strong and Courageous

I've always done my best work by following a plan: recipes, maps, calendars, itineraries, directions. I became a lifelong convert to Betty Crocker after years of hearing my mom share her recipes. My "pinches" and "little dabs" yielded quite different results from Mom's.

When my yeast rolls turned out strange, I would explain to my children, "Oh, that's from Grandma's recipe."

"Really?" was invariably their reply as they sneaked bites to the cat under the table. "Sure doesn't taste like it."

Maps? I never go anyplace I haven't been before without bringing one along. My interior compass is so imprecise that I've learned to turn directly opposite from where my instincts tell me to go. By relying on the map, I usually arrive at my appointed destination only fashionably late.

When I got married, I made similar plans. I bought a *Better Homes and Gardens* book that provided instructions for getting married: everything from the invitations to the invocations and the bouquet to the buffet. I planned it all according to the book!

Well, "the book" came through that afternoon of November 24, 1979. A lovely wedding was pulled off without a hitch. The festive occasion concluded with going home and making plans for our happily-ever-after. I planned the dinners, the decor, and the decisions to have children. Our first baby was born a couple months after our second anniversary. Then I planned her feeding time, and while she napped, I planned what her college major would be and whom she would marry.

Another daughter came along according to plan, and our son was on his way when I was stopped dead in my tracks. Suddenly *everything* was changed, and I was left *without* a plan.

Decision to Change

As I've said before, though I became a Christian early in our marriage, I had never embraced God in a personal way until my husband left me. Rather, I depended on my parents to pray for me when I encountered difficulties. But for the first time, their hot lines to God weren't sufficient. They sometimes didn't answer the phone when I called, and I felt they never understood the severity of my requests.

Days passed with swollen eyes, a broken heart, and an all-out pity party that invited anyone to come and BYOP (bring your own problems)—and many people came. I failed to hear the youthful giggles and see the excited eyes of my children, who were waiting to get on with the thrilling business of living.

One hot September afternoon in 1985, I took a walk with the horses in the field behind our home and surrendered my life to Jesus Christ. My prayer that day changed my life, though the future I faced was no less daunting.

One night some months later, in the middle of moving and going back to school, I lay on my bed feeling overwhelmed with what lay ahead. God reminded me of a familiar Scripture: "Be strong in the Lord and in his mighty power" (Galatians 6:10). I rose and looked up Bible passages about strength and found one that became my charge: "The Lord hath chosen thee to build an house for the sanctuary: be strong, and do it" (1 Chronicles 28:10, KJV).

I had heard the call. But how was I going to accomplish it? I wanted a package that held all the answers in advance and laid out the pathway I would cover over the next 10 to 15 years. I desperately longed for someone to take care of my concerns while I got a good night's sleep such as I got when I was a child. I needed a plan. A map. A recipe.

What I got instead was the Word and the command to go to God fresh every day for His manna. My dependence began to shift from my husband, parents, and self to the Lord.

In many ways, the book of Joshua provided the plan for which I was looking. It didn't supply the nice, neat, packaged answers, but it gave me a model to study for all the parenting issues I would face—this time according to *God's* plan.

Joshua's Example

Joshua was also a single parent of sorts. He had walked through the wilderness helping someone (Moses) to "bring up" some "children" (the Israelites). The book of Joshua begins when Moses had just died, and Joshua was suddenly the one in charge.

Joshua did not magically fall into the role, nor did he inherit it by default as I felt I had. He was divinely called by God to fulfill this position of leadership. Nonetheless, the "job benefits" God described to him are also available to us as single moms and dads.

• *God promised divine guidance.* "Moses my servant is dead. Now then, you and all these people, get ready to cross the Jordan River into the land I am about to give to them—to the Israelites. I will give you every place where you set your foot, as I promised Moses" (Joshua 1:2-3).

As much as Joshua missed Moses, he realized he would not be left alone in anything he did. Rather, the God who put the universe into orbit was there with a plan that included him and those he had been called to lead.

• *God promised that as long as Joshua walked with Him, he would be invincible in battle.* "No one will be able to stand up against you all the days of your life" (Joshua 1:5).

Joshua received a promise that no matter what challenges he faced, he would not be defeated. The difficulties had already been many, and countless enemies remained. Yet God assured Joshua that no matter how big or impossible the obstacles became, he would be victorious through his reliance on God.

• *God promised prosperity and success if he remained righteous.* "Do not let this Book of the Law depart from your mouth; meditate on it day and night, so that you may be careful to do everything written in it. Then you will be prosperous and successful" (Joshua 1:8).

If Joshua expected to receive the blessings of God, he must obey His commandments and walk closely with Him. Joshua had to maintain a solid relationship with the Father and grow daily through prayer and learning His statutes. If he did, God would make him successful.

• *God reminded Joshua of what he had already seen and learned about His faithfulness while with Moses.* "As I was with Moses, so I will be with you" (Joshua 1:5).

Memories came flooding back to Joshua of needs that had been met in ways that only God could have accomplished.

Finding the Answers

No doubt Joshua remembered that way back when God was first telling Moses how to structure the Hebrew nation, God had said: "Also put the Urim and the Thummim in the breastpiece, so they may be over Aaron's heart whenever he enters the presence of the Lord. Thus Aaron will always bear the means of making decisions for the Israelites over his heart before the Lord" (Exodus 28:30).

In those days, the high priest was the only person who could stand before God in the Holy of Holies. The high priests, beginning with Aaron, were responsible for hearing a need from others, going to God with the need, receiving the answer, and taking that direction back to the people.

Though the Urim and Thummim were never specifically described, many believe they were two stones that somehow gave yes or no responses to questions the people had or decisions they needed to make. Hebrew definitions offer some insight: *Urim* means "lights," and *Thummim* means "perfection" or "complete truth."

Any time Moses sought a specific direction from God concerning Israel, he could go to Aaron's Urim and Thummim for answers. And now God was handing Joshua the same tools and assurance. Every decision, problem, or challenge he would ever encounter would be answered by God.

The Job Requirements

Joshua now knew he was chosen to carry on the leadership of these people. God had provided a description of the job benefits. And what did God want from Joshua? Three times He told him in this first chapter, "Be strong and courageous" (verses 6, 7, 9).

God wanted His leader to walk forward with the goal in mind, looking neither to the right nor the left nor backward.

What was Joshua's response?

"So Joshua ordered the officers of the people" (Joshua 1:10). He took charge. God has called us as single parents to take the leadership role and move toward the goal of raising strong, courageous, godly children. He promises the same benefits to us as He did to Joshua: divine protection, guidance, victory in battle, and answers for every problem we will ever encounter—if we remain faithful.

Our job description is also the same as it was for Joshua: be strong and courageous, keep His commandments, and walk straight toward the goal. We can rest in the knowledge that though the original Urim and Thummim have long since disappeared, God's light and truth are still available for us today in the Bible and in the person of the indwelling Jesus Christ.

✄ ✄ ✄ ✄ ✄ ✄ ✄ ✄

1. Think about what you're facing today. What divine guidance do you need?

2. Which battle are you facing for which you need God's help?

3. How can God help you to become more successful?

4. Where can God fulfill His promise to make every provision you will ever need?

"Thus Aaron will always bear the means of making decisions for the Israelites over his heart before the Lord" (Exodus 28:30).

46

God's Provision for All Time

My mother has always told me we don't have to worry about things when we know the Lord, because we've already seen the end of the book. I guess I've inherited from her the love of a happy ending, and I find it through the story of Joshua.

We learned last time how God called Joshua to become a "single parent" to several million Israelites. We read about God's faithfulness to Joshua with every challenge. Now let's look at the rest of the story.

Joshua's Farewell

Joshua and the people discovered God's provision in part through the Urim and Thummim. They matured as they learned how to consult Him for all their decisions, directions, and difficulties. Through Joshua's leadership, the "kids" learned how to keep the commandments, teach their own children, wait on God, learn from mistakes, count the victories, and divide the inheritance. Joshua even remained available to help the tribes settle a civil conflict after they had all moved out on their own.

In Joshua chapters 23 and 24, he delivered his farewell address to the nation of Israel. During this speech, he reminded them of many things the Lord had done for them: "I am old and well advanced in years. You yourselves have seen everything the Lord your God has done to all these nations for your sake; it was the Lord your God who fought for you" (Joshua 23:2-3).

He told them how God would continue to go before them: "The Lord has driven out before you great and powerful nations; to this day no one has been able to withstand you. One of you routs a thousand, because the Lord your God fights for you, just as he promised. So be very careful to love the Lord your God" (23:9-11).

Joshua also exhorted them with the same words God said to him—be strong and courageous (23:6). Then Joshua said, "Choose for yourselves this day whom you will serve. . . . But as for me and my household, we will serve the Lord" (24:15).

The book of Joshua ends, and we see the litmus test of whether Joshua's words had made the desired impact. Judges is the next book in the Bible, and in Judges 1:1 we read, "After the death of Joshua, the Israelites asked the Lord . . . " They were consulting God for themselves.

Life was going on though their leader was now dead. Why? Because Joshua (and Moses before him) had equipped them to go forward with their lives and become the leaders of their own homes. And most importantly, God was still with them to guide and protect.

Plan B

God used the Urim and Thummim to answer questions through the high priest, who was the only one who could go directly to Him. But God does not tolerate sin. When the priesthood became corrupt, God stopped using it to deliver messages to His people.

Instead, God raised up prophets (along with His Word) to communicate with His people. All needs were still being supplied, and answers were still being given, but now through the prophets.

One mom in this period believed with her whole heart in God's provision. The story is found in 2 Kings 4. She lived in a town called

Shunem. The woman and her husband had prepared a room for the prophet Elisha to use when he passed through. Elisha had prayed for them to have a child, and a year later she gave birth to a son.

But then one day the unexpected happened. Their son collapsed while in the fields working with his dad. A servant brought him home. But the mother would not give up hope. She told her husband, "Please send me one of the servants and a donkey so I can go to the man of God quickly and return" (verse 22).

The husband, of course, thought she was nuts. But the woman's confident reply was, "It's all right" (verse 23). She knew that God had made a provision for His people, and she knew that provision was in the prophet Elisha.

She made her journey, and as she approached, Elisha told his servant to run and ask, "Are you all right? Is your husband all right? Is your child all right?"

The worst thing that could have happened to a mother had just occurred; her only son lay dead. Yet the very next verse reflects her faith in God's provision: "Everything is all right," she said (2 Kings 4:26).

She was correct. The prophet went back with the woman and raised her son to life. The provision had been made, and everything was all right.

The Ultimate Light and Truth

God made His greatest provision of all in the birth, life, death, and resurrection of Jesus Christ. Let's see how that affected one individual in Luke 7.

The town was again Shunem, 900 years after the time of 2 Kings. A mother, this time a widowed single mom, lost her son. Then Jesus passed through the town. "And when the Lord saw her, his heart went out to her and he said, 'Don't cry'" (verse 13).

Jesus touched the coffin and said, "'Young man . . . get up!' The dead man sat up and began to talk, and Jesus gave him back to his mother" (verses 14-15).

Once again, provision had been made. But what does that mean to you and me nearly 2,000 years later? What's the provision for us?

Hebrew 1:1-2 says, "In the past God spoke to our forefathers through the prophets at many times and in various ways, but in these last days he has spoken to us by his Son."

When Jesus died on the cross, the temple veil that separated the commoner from direct access to God was ripped apart (see Mark 15:38). From that moment on and for all generations to come, new provision was made.

The life and death of Jesus gave you and me the right to go to God for ourselves. We can consult Him for every decision we'll ever make, for every problem we'll ever encounter. Because of this provision, we can look challenges, decisions, and even death in the eye. We can go to the Father through His Son, Jesus Christ, and ask for whatever we need. Having done that, when someone asks how everything is, we can respond with the Shunammite woman's confidence, "Everything is all right."

✄ ✄ ✄ ✄ ✄ ✄ ✄ ✄

1. In what areas do you need to remember God's eternal provision today? List the problems and decisions you need to bring to God.

2. Find three people this week to whom you can proclaim, "Everything is all right." Then go about your days, doing what God has called you to do.

"In the past God spoke to our forefathers through the prophets at many times and in various ways, but in these last days he has spoken to us by his Son" (Hebrews 1:1-2).

47

Fresh Starts

I fingered through the cabinet drawer, looking for the cassette tape with a particular song. As I searched, I found a bunch of tapes—many still in their original packaging. I had purchased the tape series to help me launch a consulting career after the divorce. But I had listened only to one or two of them, and my consulting career never got off the ground.

I found the cassette I was looking for and slipped it into the player. Humming along with my favorite song, I scanned the bookshelves and saw several books I had collected while searching for direction. Some had dog-eared pages and worn bindings, while others remained shiny and untouched.

Then I spotted my wedding album and pulled it down from the shelf. I opened the pages, carefully touching the brass-tipped edges that framed happy poses of days gone by. I saw friends and relatives who had disappeared from our lives and thought about the hopes and dreams that had been shattered. I sighed, closed the album, and set aside the memories that had come flooding into my head.

I walked downstairs and out the front door, carrying my running shoes. Sitting on a step, I knocked off the mud from my last jaunt. After a quick stretch, I began my morning run.

I had learned something about running while coaching junior high girls track and participating in 10-kilometer races. I found the start of the race to be an essential part of the competition—the time when the runners line up at the starting line and watch, wait, and listen for the blast of the gun. If a runner takes off before the gun sounds, a false start is called. The runner has to go back to the line to start all over. If he or she false-starts again, that runner is disqualified from the race.

As my steps plopped on the pavement, I continued to think about the various directions my life had taken. *False starts,* I thought. *That's what my life is filled with—jumping ahead of the gun and being forced to start over again.*

The Race

Remembering the starts that had led me down dead-end or disappointing roads, I thought of the bigger race I was running. As a Christian, I was aware of more enduring issues than the ones I had been focusing on that day. The certainty of death and the question of where we will spend eternity are things we must all face. Jesus instructed us to reach the world with the gospel so that in the end, we'll bring along as many to heaven as we can. But where do we find time to witness to others when we're so consumed with schedules and plans of our own?

A Scripture comes to mind:

> Let us throw off everything that hinders and the sin that so easily entangles, and let us run with perseverance the race marked out for us. Let us fix our eyes on Jesus, the author and perfecter of our faith, who for the joy set before him endured the cross, scorning its shame, and sat down at the right hand of the throne of God. Consider him who endured such opposition from sinful men, so that you will not grow weary and lose heart. (Hebrews 12:1-3)

The race marked out for us. With all the mistakes and false starts I've experienced, it's hard to believe there's a course for me to follow. But my course has been designed just for me, and it incorporates all the turns I've taken along the way—both good and bad. God knew what my decisions and experiences would be when He mapped out my specific race.

Even knowing that, however, it's difficult to let go of my own goals and agendas, because I bring along interests, ambitions, concerns, and memories that slow me down en route to the finish line.

I've known swimmers who didn't shave their legs until the day of the meet so they would get the closest shave possible. They knew that even the tiny hairs on their legs could keep them from achieving their best time. If something so small can impede their best efforts, what about the bigger things in my life?

To the Finish

Several summers ago, my mother went to California to attend my brother Jason's graduation from Army boot camp. When the ceremony was over, Mom had to wait two more days before taking him home on leave. Jason, sensing my mother's concern about the delay, said, "Mom, it's not long—just two more days and then a wake-up!"

Later that same summer, my son was visiting his father just before the start of kindergarten. I talked to my son one day on the phone. "Mom, how many more days till I get home?" he asked.

"Just two more," I answered.

"How many more dark times is that?" Clint asked.

"Two," I whispered. "Only two."

The first day of school came. That afternoon, I waited in our yard for the bus to arrive at the corner and release my children. I couldn't wait to hear all their first-day-of-school stories.

Clint stepped off the bus, and I could see a smile spread across his face as soon as he looked toward home. He started running, gaining speed with every step. He threw off his book bag and dropped his jacket, never losing a stride until he jumped into my arms and embraced me with a hug. "I'm so glad to be home!" he said.

Shouldn't I run my race the same way Clint ran to me that day? Don't I need to forget what lies behind? Shouldn't I throw off everything I find that's slowing me down—worries, memories, plans—as Clint did his book bag, and keep my eyes on Jesus?

None of us knows how many more dark times there will be before we get home. But there's much to do—lives to reach and children to raise for God. One day, for all of us, there's going to be a wake-up call, and we need to be ready.

No matter how many mistakes or wrong turns we've taken, God is the master of *fresh* starts. How we began the race is not as important to God as how we end it.

I rounded the corner from my morning run. Home was in sight. Suddenly I felt a new surge of energy. I held my head high and ran confidently forward with my eyes on the goal.

And then I heard myself saying, "Thank You, Lord, for being a God of fresh starts."

Hebrews 11 showcases great heroes of faith from the Bible. Many of them knew what it means to experience false starts. As you read through that chapter, especially verses 13-16, consider what qualities you can cultivate as well.

※　※　※　※　※　※　※　※

1. They lived by faith and believed in the promises of God, no matter what the circumstances.

What have you done that makes you feel like a failure? What circumstances in your life cause you to doubt God is in control?

2. They held loosely to the things of this world—material belongings, status, and achievements.

What are you holding onto that interferes with your walk with God?

3. They searched for something better and more enduring.

What long-range goals does God want you to embrace that will matter for eternity?

4. They forgot what lay behind them so they wouldn't be tempted to return to it.

What false starts do you need to let go of? What's keeping you from looking up to God, the creator of fresh starts?

"Let us run with perseverance the race marked out for us" (Hebrews 12:1).

48

Hearing His Voice

I stuck an old tape in the tape player one day and heard these words sung by Cynthia Clawson:

> All things work for our good,
> though sometimes we can't see how they could.
> Struggles that break our hearts in two
> sometimes blind us to the truth.
> Our Father knows what's best for us;
> His ways are not our own.
> So when your pathway grows dim
> and you just can't see Him,
> Remember, you're never alone.
> God is too wise to be mistaken.
> God is too good to be unkind.
> So when you don't understand,
> when you don't see His plan
> When you can't trace His hand, trust His heart.

(Copyright 1989 by May Sun Music and Causing Change Music [both admin. by Word Entertainment, Inc.], Word Music, and Dayspring Music [both divisions of Word Entertainment, Inc.]. All rights reserved. Used by permission.)

As I heard the words, I flashed back to 1990 and the couch at a friend's house where I first heard the song. I was on my way to my doctoral hooding ceremony. What I was going to do next? Where would I work? How would I hear God's direction?

Moving back to the present, I remembered events that have brought me where I am today, and I recognized each move as a fingerprint of God. I didn't know how God would accomplish these moves, but I was certain He would. I had seen Him answer too many prayers and give too many directions when I was a child and after my commitment to Him. But *how* had I heard His voice through the years?

The Unusual Direct Approach

God's direction doesn't normally come through the intercom or the mail. The story found in Daniel 5 is highly unusual in this regard. The ungodly King Belshazzar of Babylon received some good news and some bad news one night. The good news was that he heard directly from God through God's handwriting on the wall. The bad news was that he only lived long enough to see it once.

Belshazzar was having a big party for a thousand of his nobles. He drank wine with them and gave orders to bring in the gold and silver goblets that his father, Nebuchadnezzar, had stolen from the temple in Jerusalem.

They were drinking from the goblets when fingers appeared and wrote a message on the palace's plastered wall. Belshazzar was so scared that his knees knocked together. He got Daniel to interpret the words of God's displeasure with him, and that night the words came true—King Belshazzar died.

I've never seen God write His message on the wall. I've never heard Him speak audibly to my ears. I have, however, "heard" His words and "seen" His messages in other ways, and I've found them reliable thus far.

He Speaks Through Circumstances

God has a way of getting His point across by events that occur. Once when I was a senior in college, my younger sister went with me to a business that was hiring college students for the summer. The company would select one person as a summer secretary making $12 per hour— a fortune to us at the time. If I took classes through the summer, I could graduate in December, but I was out of money. So working through the summer would pay for the rest of my schooling and enable me to graduate in March.

I was highly qualified for the job, so I waited confidently to hear from the company. One week passed, then two, and the first day of summer classes arrived. I was depressed as I realized I wasn't enrolled in classes *or* working at a well-paying summer job. I sat at my desk at the part-time, low-paying job I *did* have and cried.

Then I received two phone calls. One was from my mom saying the business had called *my sister* to come to work for them. The other was from the dean of my college. He wanted me to do some research for him. "And oh, by the way," he said, "my wife sent you some certificates she has collected from her student teachers for free university classes."

The next day, my sister went to work, and I made my way to classes and to the dean's office, where I gathered enough certificates to finish my degree at no cost—by December.

Those circumstances left nothing to decide—no choice. I knew I was doing what God wanted by the way He worked out the details.

He Speaks Through People

When my children and I began attending our church in Ohio, I asked God for a place to work in the church that would fit with my busy schedule. I didn't need to care for more children in the nursery, Thursday choir practice was impossible, and teaching a Sunday school class was out of the question. Then a lady asked my children and me to join a group doing inner-city outreach.

We went on a Saturday to the soup kitchen—and then on many Saturdays that followed. Soon we developed a ritual on Thanksgiving Day of baking a turkey and going to feed the homeless before coming back to our own family meal. We had found a place where we could get involved together while sharing what God had given us. As a result of that woman's invitation, we got clear direction from God for a family ministry.

He Speaks Through Our Seeking

A friend once told me he thought it was easier to stay in God's will than to get out of it when we sincerely search for His direction.

When I first became a single mom, my children had never had any vaccinations. I had been terrified by reports of what could happen through these inoculations. But my oldest was starting kindergarten, and the only way I could avoid having her inoculated was to sign papers stating it was against my religion, which it wasn't. I was confused at the time over how many of my feelings were true reactions to the issues and how many were reactions against my husband, who endorsed inoculations. I prayed, "God, I don't want to make the wrong decision out of spite. Please show me what to do."

As the time drew near to make the decision, I began to beg for writing on the wall. The first day of school came. I had no answer. I remember praying as I drove my daughter to the doctor to get that first shot: "God, I'm doing the best I know. Please honor that, keep my heart right, and protect my daughter from all harm."

That was many years ago, and all my kids' inoculation records are now up to date. You won't find three healthier children anywhere.

He Speaks Through Our Instincts

I've learned not to rely totally on my feelings. But sometimes God uses them to get across His message.

Several months after moving into our first apartment as a single-parent family, I got the feeling that I was supposed to buy a house. That wasn't something I wanted to do yet, however, as I didn't even have time to change a light bulb, much less mow a lawn.

Nonetheless, I sincerely asked God to open the doors if it was His will. I called a real estate agent I knew (not knowing if they would work with a single graduate-student mom making $7,600 a year) and asked her to talk to me about houses. She did. And within the month, we were in a house that became home for my three children and me for the next seven years—at a lower cost than our rent had been.

He Speaks Through His Word

No matter what other ways I've found to hear God's voice, I make sure what I'm hearing is consistent with the Bible. All instruction should line up with what the Bible teaches, because God never contradicts Himself. I never proceed with my decisions until this confirmation is made.

Once my ex-husband was taking me back to court. I was deeply involved with my doctoral classes, so I had little time to talk to God about it. But fear gripped me for weeks preceding the court date.

The morning I had to go to court, I prayed, "God, I've been so busy. I don't know what to say when I get before the judge. I'm scared."

Then I opened my Bible to Luke 12:11: "When you are brought before synagogues, rulers and authorities, do not worry about how you will defend yourselves or what you will say, for the Holy Spirit will teach you at that time what you should say."

And He did. When I got to court, my ex-husband dropped the case he was trying to make. I watched God work in my behalf in everything that concerned me.

Finding His Fingerprints

One summer my children and I took a vacation through Minnesota and across South Dakota. The lakes in Minnesota were breathtaking, and the Badlands and Mount Rushmore made vivid memories in my mind. When we got home, I highlighted on our road map the exact route we had taken. That map took its place beside our photos of the wonderful vacation and reminded us each time we looked at them of the paths we had followed.

Reviewing my journey of decisions as a Christian, I can likewise trace the workings of God. The more I've been able to recognize His fingerprints in my directions, the less I need to actually see His handwriting on the wall. The more I see His workmanship, the less I need to see Him *at* work. My ears have grown attuned and my heart receptive to anything He wishes to say.

Isaiah 30:21 says, "Whether you turn to the right or to the left, your ears will hear a voice behind you, saying, 'This is the way; walk in it.'"

That voice may come through circumstances, people, seeking, instincts, His Word, or still other ways, but God has His methods of getting His points across. He's just looking for ears willing to hear and hearts willing to obey those instructions. Knowing that He wants us to hear His voice more than we want to hear it gives me confidence. It helps me to remember that even when I don't understand or see His plan—when I can't trace His hand—I can still trust His heart.

❈ ❈ ❈ ❈ ❈ ❈ ❈ ❈

1. List some good decisions you've made since you've known Christ. Describe the method God used to speak to you.

2. Name places where you goofed up. Where did you fail to hear from Him?

3. What can you do to better hear that gentle voice behind you saying, "This is the way"?

"I will guide you in the way of wisdom and lead you along straight paths" (Proverbs 4:11).

49

The Teen Thing

I once heard someone say, "My daughter will be 15 in May—if I let her live that long."

I didn't understand the thinking behind those words until I had teens of my own. Then I found it necessary to scrap most of the parenting techniques I had hammered out and forge into uncharted waters. Out came every book on the topic of raising teens that I could find. Once I even wrote a letter to one of my daughters, borrowing some of the words from a book of Dr. James Dobson's that lay open beside me on the bed.

Loss of control seems to be the biggest issue I wrestle with in raising my teens. Never in my parenting had I felt I wasn't making direct contact—maintaining a firm grasp—until this phase. But in all these things, God is showing me how to let go of the things I can't control and concentrate on the things I *can* change. Guess who that change involves? My teens? No, their mother, me.

I can no longer dictate what my children will wear or eat or how they'll fix their hair. I can choose, however, how I'll respond to their choices and how I'll guide them in the decisions they make. That releases me from my self-imposed need to "fix" things and gives me back control of the issues I can do something about.

Today I'm a few miles into the journey of raising my teens. The road has been bumpy and has presented some hairpin turns and narrow escapes along the way. But as I seek guidance from God for this awesome task, I continue to find Him faithful.

Fruits of Our Labors

When you and I became heads of our homes, we took on a similar role to that of the high priest in the Old Testament. He was the one who would go into the Holy of Holies, offer sacrifices, and represent the people to God.

The high priest's blue robe was carefully crafted, as described in detail in Exodus 39:25-26. On the hem were strands of yarn formed like the pomegranate fruit. The pomegranates acted as pads between a row of bells that were made of hand-beaten gold, each offering its own unique sound. The soft fabric of the pomegranates kept the bells from striking each other. The bells were free to ring their own sounds, chiming together in harmony, but the pomegranates kept them from striking against each other in discord.

C. Paul Willis, in his book *Bells and Pomegranates,* said this alternating bell and pomegranate configuration on the priest's robe can be likened to the gifts and fruit in our lives.

The gifts are listed in 1 Corinthians 12:8-10: "To one there is given through the Spirit the message of wisdom, to another the message of knowledge . . . to another faith . . . to another gifts of healing . . . to another miraculous powers . . . to another prophecy, to another distinguishing between spirits, to another speaking in different tongues, and to still another the interpretation of tongues."

In Galatians 5:22-23, we read about the "fruit of the Spirit." This fruit depicts certain character qualities that we can take on in our growth as children of God: "love, joy, peace, patience, kindness, goodness, faithfulness, gentleness and self-control."

All of us as moms and dads are gifted in various ways— vocationally, emotionally, and spiritually. Whether we teach our children how to solve a complicated math problem or how to fix a car, we pass on the skills and interests that we ourselves possess. But if we don't share these things in the right way, no matter how talented we are or how good our intentions, we will meet resistance from our kids.

The Bible says it this way: "If I speak in the tongues of men and of angels, but have not love, I am only a resounding gong or a clanging cymbal. If I have the gift of prophecy and can fathom all mysteries and all knowledge, and if I have a faith that can move mountains, but have not love, I am nothing. If I give all I possess to the poor and surrender my body to the flames, but have not love, I gain nothing" (1 Corinthians 13:1-3).

Fertilizing Our Fruit

The more fruit we grow, the more effectively we can use our gifts. So how can we make ourselves accountable for developing this fruit? Let's look at the different aspects individually.

• *Love* represents the nature of God. It's defined in 1 Corinthians 13 by its attributes: "Love is patient . . . kind . . . does not envy, it does not boast, it is not proud. It is not rude, it is not self-seeking, it is not easily angered, it keeps no record of wrongs. Love does not delight in evil but rejoices with the truth. It always protects, always trusts, always hopes, always perseveres. Love never fails" (verses 4-8).

Unconditional love for our teens must be evident at all times. They should be certain that our love for them will never change and is not dependent on their behavior.

• *Joy* is often equated with happiness, but the two are quite different. Happiness depends on happenings—sunny weather, timely child-support checks, good health. Happiness and unhappiness do not exist together, but joy and sorrow do.

God didn't promise us happiness, but He did promise we could know joy. It's joy that brings a smile in the midst of a deep valley or unhappy news. When we have it, our children know it. Joy shows on our faces, in our walk, and in the things we say. Joy is our silent witness to the confidence we hold in God.

• *Peace* shows itself through a calmness during tough times. I get opportunities to exhibit this quality when new trials arise. "No, the money isn't here yet, but it will be okay," I assure my kids. Peace becomes an outward indicator of an inward conviction that God is in charge of all things.

• *Patience* is best developed under trials (see James 1:3-4; 5:11). Telling our kids about it will never get our point across. They must see patience alive and well as we work through our own issues. Our teenagers will push us sometimes to see how far this patience will extend. But the patience that God gives knows no boundaries.

• *Kindness* is shown through our affection, sympathy, and helpfulness. One day my children and I were pulling away from a bank, and we saw a woman with a child on her back begging for money. I rounded the block and returned to share a little that we had. I realized the woman's claim of need may have been a hoax, but the kindness I displayed in front of my kids was not. That made it worth the gamble.

• *Goodness* is doing the right thing even when it's not the easy or the comfortable thing to do. It's an active approach, not just a passive refraining from acting badly. If goodness is lacking, even in little things, people notice.

I'm reminded of the story of the woman who dumped all the yucky things happening to her on the other occupants of the bus she rode. As she got off, a voice called to her, "Lady, you left something behind."

"Oh, yeah?" she responded. "What's that?"

"A very bad impression" was the reply.

Our goodness is a reflection (albeit a dim one) of God's holiness. Since His commitment is to conform us to the image of His holy Son (see Romans 8:29), we can be sure He's willing and eager to help us grow in this aspect of the Spirit's fruit.

• *Faithfulness* implies loyalty, constancy, and freedom from fickleness (see 2 Corinthians 1:18, Galatians 5:22, 2 Timothy 2:2). Our teens need to know we'll be there for them no matter what. They learn this as they watch us be faithful to our employers, our friends, and especially God. Every time they see us write a check and drop our offering in the collection plate, they see faithfulness. When they see us keep a secret, they see faithfulness. Faithfulness tells them there are some things and some people who are worth sticking by, no matter what.

• *Gentleness* is the opposite of harshness, sternness, or violence. I often repeat the Scripture that talks about the unfading beauty of a gentle and quiet spirit (see 1 Peter 3:4). When dealing with teens, gentleness is often hard to maintain. But I've seen God control the ugliness of a harsh response I wanted to make and replace it with a gentle answer that brought about an unfading beauty in me. I've learned time and again how a gentle answer stops anger (see Proverbs 15:1).

• *Self-control* is the restraint exercised on one's own impulses, emotions, or desires. Our teens need to see us in control of all aspects of our existence—from how we spend money to how we handle our anger, fear, and loneliness. When we exercise self-control, it tells our children that we can do all things through Christ who strengthens us (see Philippians 4:13). That, in turn, will help them develop their own self-control.

It's Up to Us

We have an awesome job, parents. Our kids' teen years compose the last major leg of the parenting journey. Our children deserve a "high priest" worthy of that calling.

When I was a child, we had a section on our property where we grew strawberries, raspberries, grapes, and peaches. My brothers and sisters and I enjoyed those fresh fruits through spring and summer, and then the frozen fruits when the snows fell.

I took those delicious fruits for granted until I was much older and recognized the correlation between those bountiful harvests and my dad and mom's hard work. The pruning, weeding, hoeing, and picking didn't happen on their own.

Just about the best way we can help our teens is to cooperate with the Holy Spirit as He grows His fruit in us. The more they see that modeled in us, the more their own fruit is likely to develop. We must show rather than just tell—love, joy, peace, patience, kindness, goodness, faithfulness, gentleness, and self-control. Our example will ripen their hearts so that they'll want to see a rich harvest in their own lives as well.

❄ ❄ ❄ ❄ ❄ ❄ ❄ ❄

1. Think of your responses to your teen during the past two weeks. How have you measured up in the fruit department? Give specific positive or negative examples of the following.

Love:

Joy:

Peace:

Patience:

Kindness:

Goodness:

Faithfulness:

Gentleness:

Self-control:

2. Now prune that fruit! List ways you can more effectively respond to your teen.

"Let us hold unswervingly to the hope we profess, for he who promised is faithful. And let us consider how we may spur one another on toward love and good deeds" (Hebrews 10:23-24).

50

Big Things in
Little Places

I grew up as one of eight children, living with my mom and dad in a small Ohio town. After the first week of December each year, the local college dismissed for Christmas break, which was a kind of signal for my sisters, brothers, and me. Our parents would drive us through town, and we would select our family tree from the ones prematurely pitched out by students in the dormitories. I can still see the pines and spruces leaning against the trash cans, the used tinsel glistening in the sun. Year after year, the throwaway tree we selected became the center of our family festivities.

One Christmas morning is fixed in my memory. Our family was seated around the secondhand tree, which that year consumed more than half our living room. A crooked star was perched on top, where the tree had been cut to clear our low ceiling. Dad assumed his role of announcing the names on the packages and then passing them out. Some he slid across the linoleum floor.

It was always an exciting time, but that year the thrill of what was in store for me was dashed when I didn't hear my name. Ignored in the activity, I watched my brothers and sisters as they ripped the wrapping from their boxes. I bit my lip to hold back the tears. Then Dad saw another present under the tree. "Looks like we forgot one here," he said as he handed me an unusually small package.

What? That's all? I thought as he laid the box on the palm of my hand. It was so tiny that the label with my name stuck over the side. I blinked my eyes in disappointment as I remembered how tight money was in our family, especially that year when the house needed repairs.

The wrapping paper came off, and a white box now shook in my hand as I lifted the lid and gazed inside. There on a flat square of cotton was the most beautiful silver charm bracelet I had ever seen. A heavy chain that fit exactly around my wrist held two glistening charms—an angel and a heart that said, "I love you."

I couldn't talk. I had wanted a charm bracelet like those of the other girls at school, but I thought we could never afford one. As my mother reached over to help me fasten the latch, I threw my arms around both my parents. "Thank you!" I almost shouted. "Oh, Daddy and Mommy, thank you!"

I can't remember what the others got that Christmas morning. But I can still see the sunlight reflecting off my long-awaited charm bracelet as it dangled delicately from my wrist.

I've opened other "little boxes" throughout my life to find big truths inside—all of which I needed and some of which I had wanted for a long time. Those presents came unexpectedly, when God spoke through the ordinary, often difficult events in my life. I discovered such a box one recent Christmas.

Lesson in the Snow

My children and I had just experienced our first Christmas in Colorado. A few days afterward, we drove a couple of hours to Copper Mountain for their first skiing in the Rockies. It's a huge mountain, much different from the small Ohio hills they had learned on and where we spent 30 minutes in line and 30 seconds skiing down.

The day was crisp and brilliant. On the chair lift, I sat between my daughter Ashley, 12, and Clint, my eight-year-old son. We soon arrived at the top and were adjusting our poles when Ashley, impatient to show her ability and independence, announced that she would meet us at the bottom. I watched with some concern as she confidently pushed forward and skied out of sight.

Clint, meanwhile, was staring wide-eyed at the slope before him. "I haven't skied for a long time, Mom," he reminded me in a low voice.

"Just follow me," I said.

Moving several feet down the mountain, I turned to watch him do the same. His tips were close and his legs were spread in the familiar snowplow stance as he tried to follow in my tracks. But he soon fell, and fresh snow covered his face as he started to cry. "I'm scared," he said. "I can't do this. I don't want to go the rest of the way down."

"Sure, you can do it," I assured him. "I'll be right beside you, and we'll take as much time as you need to go down."

I helped him up, dusted the snow from his pants legs, and wiped the last tear from his cold cheek. I couldn't help but realize how much he had grown since the times I picked him up when he was learning to ride his bike. And I couldn't help but wonder about how often he would need me after falls in the years to come.

We continued down the trail. Small clumps of snow dropped from the trees and landed in the powder at our feet. Clint moved mechanically down the slope, his face quietly saying, *Are we having fun yet?*

I looked back to where we had come from and forward to where we were going. And at that moment, I realized I had discovered yet another big gift in a little box. My role as a mom was being summed up in this simple trip down a mountainside.

• *I guided.* I showed Clint the path to take that would get him to the bottom most quickly and with the least chance of harm. The choices were many, but we needed to stay on the easy paths marked for us. I knew which trails were appropriate for our abilities. I modeled discretion by choosing the right paths, and Clint followed.

• *I protected.* Trees lined both sides of the trail, and skilled skiers and snowboarders flew by us. I kept Clint far enough to the side so he wouldn't obstruct others, but not so close to the side that he could crash into the trees.

• *I encouraged.* No one knew the little boy on that slope the way I did, and no one had a greater opportunity to support and uplift him. "You can do it!" "Good job!" "That was great!" were some of the expressions he heard. I couldn't help but wonder how far he would have gone if he had heard, "You clumsy ox!" "How stupid!" "Can't you do anything right?"

• *I taught independence.* Clint was careful at first to follow in my tracks. But the farther down the mountain we moved, the more he gained confidence and made tracks of his own. He did fall again near the bottom, but when I skied up to him and asked if he needed help, he said, "I'm okay, Mom. I can get it."

Down at the chair lift, Ashley stood waiting for us. She told me she would be riding back up with a girl she had met coming down and would catch up with us later. I squinted into the sun as I watched Clint finish his run. "Come on, Mom," he said when he arrived. "I want to ride back up. Can't we go any faster?"

I smiled and moved toward the lift. This time Clint was in the lead. I realized that in the years to come, his tracks would become larger than mine, and he would choose paths far different from those I walked. But I also sensed he would always have a place in his heart for

Someone who would be there with him in his challenges to guide, protect, and encourage him.

From lessons like the one on that mountainside, Clint has come to know the truth of Hebrews 13:5 about a Father who says, "Never will I leave you; never will I forsake you." And from those same lessons, I've learned to believe in Proverbs 22:6: "Train a child in the way he should go, and when he is old he will not turn from it." I know that Clint is now choosing daily the way *he should go.* What a wonderful gift to discover in such a tiny box!

1. What big things have you found in "little boxes" in recent months?

2. God has much He longs to teach us. Life experience, coupled with an intimate knowledge of Him, allows us to hear and think as He would. But our ears must be tuned in and our faith founded on the truth of God's Word. Otherwise, we can hear the wrong voices.

What messages might God be speaking to you today?

"Apply your heart to instruction and your ears to words of knowledge" (Proverbs 23:12).

51

A Firm Place

Six-year-old Ashley sat on the step and played with some lint on the carpet. I stepped over her, my arms loaded with clothes to put away. The divorce was almost final, and the children and I had just moved into an apartment in another state.

"Ashley," I said, "why don't you go outside and play?"

"I don't know anyone to play with," she replied.

"Then go upstairs, unpack your dolls, and play with them till I finish a few of these jobs."

"I don't want to play with my dolls," she retorted.

I closed the closet door, then turned, almost falling over her as she stood close to my heels.

"Ashley!" I yelled. "I must get these things unpacked and get ready to go back to work tomorrow. Please either help or go swing in the backyard."

"That swing is all yucky," she said. "Why can't we go back home and swing on *my* swing set? I don't like this apartment. I don't like our neighbors. Why did we have to get divorced?" She fell into my arms, sobbing.

I slid down the wall onto the floor and held Ashley close. "Sometimes things just happen, sweetheart," I said. "No one is ever prepared for these kinds of things."

The weight of the divorce felt heavier on my shoulders. How would

I be able to do all the things Ashley's father used to do—mow the lawn, wash the car, play ball—plus all the cooking and cleaning?

"Sweetheart," I reassured her, "you know we have the Lord. He helps His children through everything."

"But Mommy," Ashley said, "this is too much, even for God. Why did this all have to happen?"

"Ashley, come with me," I said, leading her down the hall.

Something to Be Certain About

We went into my bedroom. "What do we have here?" I asked, pointing to the pictures on the bed that were waiting to be hanged.

"Pictures. Do we have to hang them now?" she asked.

I ignored Ashley's question and picked up the picture on top. A small box of nails and a hammer lay nearby.

"Does this look all right here?" I asked, stepping onto a chair and holding the picture against the wall.

"I guess so," she answered.

"Hand me the hammer and a nail."

I tapped the nail gently into the wall and hung the picture over the bureau. Then I climbed down from the chair and reclined across the bed, facing the picture.

"You know," I said, "the nail we just put in that wall will fall out if something too heavy is hung on it. But in houses that were built a long time ago, rows of large nails or pegs were placed in the walls for keeps. They wouldn't come out unless the walls were torn down."

Ashley lay down beside me.

"On these pegs, " I continued, "all kinds of things were hung— trophies, shields, swords, gold and silver cups, and changes of clothes that belonged to the members of the family."

I pulled my Bible from the drawer in the table beside the bed. "In the book of Isaiah," I said, "there was a man named Eliakim. God chose him for a job in a high court and gave him this promise: 'I will drive him like a peg into a firm place; he will be a seat of honor for the house of his father. All the glory of his family will hang on him: its offspring and offshoots—all its lesser vessels, from the bowls to all the jars'" (Isaiah 22:23-24).

"What does that have to do with us, Mommy?" Ashley asked.

I turned to face her. "Just like Eliakim, when God chooses someone to take over a job, all the glory of that house is hung on that chosen one. That person won't perish, nor will that family's concerns fall to the ground, however big they may be. In our family, by faith, we've hung our concerns on Jesus. He's our peg in a firm place.

"Because of that," I said with assurance, "we'll be able to take whatever comes up, and nothing that comes our way will fall to the ground. Do you understand?"

"Yes, I think I do," said Ashley. She stood up, her look of concern gone for now. "Mommy, can I go outside and play?"

"Yeah, in a minute," I said, ruffling her hair. "But first help me put up a couple more of these pictures."

Afterward, we walked together to the front door. Ashley put on her jacket and opened the door, stopping to look at her reflection in the glass of a picture hanging in the hallway. She turned and looked at me and said, "You know, everything's going to be okay."

I sat down on the step and watched her close the door. "I know," I whispered. "I know."

Time-Proven

A number of years have passed since I first shared that promise with Ashley. Though I sounded strong and sure of myself, I, too, was a scared little girl whose only choices were to worry or to be assured that what my Father told me was true.

A day doesn't go by in which I don't have the opportunity to trust in

God. Not only is that true for me, but it's true for Ashley as well.

When she was 11, something happened to upset her during a visit with her father. He's not a Christian, and he challenged her faith severely. She ran crying to her room at his house and closed the door. Then she, following her mom's example, reached for her Bible for direction.

That young girl's Bible opened to 2 Timothy 3, which talks about evidences of sin in the last days before the return of Christ. And then she read: "But as for you, continue in what you have learned and have become convinced of, because you know of those from whom you learned it, and how from infancy you have known the holy Scriptures, which are able to make you wise for salvation through faith in Christ Jesus" (verses 14-15).

God was instructing her directly. He knew where she was and what she needed at that very moment. And beyond what happened that day, Ashley was assured one more time that nothing she would ever encounter would be too hard for her to handle through God. Nothing.

Today, Ashley and I are still being reminded that He not only calls us for service, but He also equips us for each and every task. We're learning that all we need to do is live our lives for Him, move forward to what He has called us to do, and then rest in His complete ability to care for it all.

⚜ ⚜ ⚜ ⚜ ⚜ ⚜ ⚜ ⚜

Do you have issues today that concern you? Take a few moments and do three things:

1. Assess your life, and see if there's any sin that stands between you and God. If there is, ask for forgiveness.

2. Lay out all your concerns. Tell God the things that bother you today.

3. Recite those words from Isaiah: "I will drive him like a peg into a firm place; he will be a seat of honor for the house of his father." Now rest in that place.

"May the God of peace . . . equip you with everything good for doing his will, and may he work in us what is pleasing to him, through Jesus Christ, to whom be glory for ever and ever" (Hebrews 13:20-21).

52

Learning to Lean

I was visiting with my parents in a southern Arizona border town in 1977. The welcome rains of August had touched the arid brown of the desert, anointing it and turning it into visions of green, mesquite-covered hills. The tumbleweed dotted the prairie with symmetrical bouquets, while white sage and lavender verbena grew in a carpet beneath.

The freshness of the day brought the spicy fragrance of the desert acacia bushes through the open windows of the small church where my dad and I were seated for the early morning service. From where I sat, fingers of the morning sun pulled colors of purples, grays, and greens from the far mountains. Their peaks were wreathed in clouds that slowly lifted the way a stage curtain parts to reveal the next act of a play. I was not aware that a new day was dawning in my life as well.

Looking Back

I was single, just out of college, and working at my first job. Life was going well for me, and my future looked bright. I had become engaged to a man who knew nothing about a personal relationship with Jesus Christ. But I never thought I would need the Lord any more than I seemed to need Him then, which wasn't much. Besides, if I got in trouble, I would just call Mom and Dad, who would pray and move God in my behalf.

My parents had maintained a close walk with the Lord throughout my growing-up years. I had seen their prayers answered and blessings received. As a result, I found myself depending on their prayers for decisions I had to make and hard times I was forced to endure—just as I depended on them for oatmeal cake.

Let me explain. Since I was a child, my mother had baked this favorite cake for my birthday. After I married, she continued to do so. One day it dawned on me that if I were going to keep eating oatmeal cake, I was going to have to learn the recipe myself. Mom wouldn't always be available, as they were preparing to move from their Ohio home to Arizona.

The same was true about my faith. If I were going to continue enjoying the blessings of answered prayer, I needed to learn the "recipe" myself. I grew hungry for a personal relationship with Jesus.

Back to Reality

I was jerked back from my reverie in the church beside my dad as the congregation began to sing an unfamiliar song, "Learning to Lean":

> I'm learning to lean, learning to lean,
> Learning to lean on Jesus.
> Finding more power than I'd ever dreamed;
> I'm learning to lean on Jesus.

Then these words jumped out at me:

> The joy I can't explain fills my soul,
> Since the day I made Jesus my King.
> His blessed Holy Spirit is leading my way;
> He's teaching and I'm learning to lean.

I stopped singing and looked ahead at the rest of the words:

There's glorious victory each day now for me,
I found His peace so serene;
He helps me with each task if only I'll ask;
Every day now I'm learning to lean.

(© 1976 HeartWarming Music. All rights reserved. Used by permission.)

I lay the hymnal down long after the song had ended and looked at my father. He sat with his eyes closed, his index finger between his eyes, propping his head. Suddenly I knew. It was time that *I* learned to lean on God. I had always leaned on my parents, who had leaned on Him. Now it was time for me to learn to lean.

And a good thing it was.

Years of trials, decisions, and difficulties followed. My parents were gone and handling problems of their own. Eventually I became a single mom of three babies. During those days of desperation, it was not great sums of money from my parents that helped. I turned to the Lord they had introduced me to and made Him the Lord not only of those circumstances, but also of my whole life. And what has that meant to me?

• *"Finding more power than I ever dreamed."* I'm now far less fearful when I run into new problems. The One who is all-powerful is with me all the time to guide me through rough waters. He has been faithful in the past; He'll remain faithful for what lies ahead. "You are awesome, O God, in your sanctuary; the God of Israel gives power and strength to his people" (Psalm 68:35). "He gives strength to the weary and increases the power of the weak" (Isaiah 40:29).

• *"The joy I can't explain fills my soul."* Have the hardships ceased? No way! But only those who know God can understand the joy that comes in the midst of darkness. Only God can bring a song to a broken heart and a smile to a sad face. "Gladness and joy will overtake them, and sorrow and sighing will flee away" (Isaiah 35:10).

• *"I found His peace so serene."* Leaning on God doesn't eliminate our problems, but it gives us incredible peace as He guides us safely through them. His peace is there for the taking. "You will keep in perfect peace him whose mind is steadfast, because he trusts in you" (Isaiah 26:3).

• *"He helps me with each task if only I'll ask."* One afternoon I had a bad headache. The last thing I felt like doing was taking my young children to midweek service, along with two kids from the neighborhood. But I did it. I dropped them off, then pulled into a place in the parking lot. I leaned my head back and prayed for my sickness—for the first time that day. Before I got the words out of my mouth, my headache and nausea were gone. Then I knew that God had wanted to help me with this difficulty much earlier, but He had wanted me to ask. "Ask and it will be given to you; seek and you will find; knock and the door will be opened to you. For everyone who asks receives; he who seeks finds; and to him who knocks, the door will be opened" (Matthew 7:7-8).

"He's teaching and I'm learning to lean."

Sitting in that Arizona church in 1977, I didn't know what lay ahead for me on the long road toward learning to lean on Jesus. But now I've had 20 years of discovering what it means to know Him as my living Lord and guide. Each day holds new experiences that provide new lessons as I learn to lean.

✖ ✖ ✖ ✖ ✖ ✖ ✖ ✖

Make this the day that you begin to lean more on God. As you learn to do that, you and God will be able to get through anything.

"He gives strength to the weary and increases the power of the weak" (Isaiah 40:29).